What the
**Science
of Reading**
Says
about

Reading
Comprehension and
Content Knowledge

Jennifer Jump, M.A., and Kathleen Kopp, M.S.Ed.

MW00558867

Annotation	When to Use It
underline	main idea
circle	key words
!	very important

Other Books in This Series

Contributing Author

Carrie Eicher, M.A.Ed.
Port Charlotte, Florida

Contributors

Christina Castanos
Elementary Science Coordinator, Clint, Texas
Kimberly Saguilan
Former Principal, Santa Ana, California
Lisa Callahan
Former Director of Literacy, Wheaton, Illinois

Image Credits: all images Shutterstock and/or iStock

Publishing Credits

Corinne Burton, M.A.Ed., *Publisher*
Aubrie Nielsen, M.S.Ed., *EVP of Content Development*
Emily R. Smith, M.A.Ed., *SVP of Content Development*
Véronique Bos, *VP of Creative*
Cathy Hernandez, *Senior Content Manager*
Jill Malcolm, *Graphic Designer*
David Slayton, *Assistant Editor*

Shell Education

A division of Teacher Created Materials
5482 Argosy Avenue
Huntington Beach, CA 92649
www.tcmpub.com/shell-education
ISBN 978-1-0876-9670-6
© 2023 Shell Educational Publishing, Inc.

Table of Contents

Table of Contents *(cont.)*

Table of Contents *(cont.)*

Introduction

Welcome from Jen Jump

The Hippocratic oath is powerful. Most of us have heard it spoken of, usually in passing, perhaps while watching a medical drama on television. We often think of the oath in terms of the simple phrase "Do no harm." The reality is that the oath is much more substantive. The language is intense, lofty, and powerful. According to tradition, medical professionals have been swearing some form of the Hippocratic oath since the fourth century BCE. Without parsing out the implications and utility of the oath to modern-day medicine, most people know its purpose and relevance.

The current version of the oath (revised in 1964) articulates several thoughtful tenets that stand out:

1. **I will respect the hard-won scientific gains of those physicians in whose steps I walk, and gladly share such knowledge as is mine with those who are to follow.**

    Yes! I want every doctor I meet to listen to the knowledge gained from the physicians who went before them. I want my medical professionals to share what they learn from diagnosing and treating me. In the same way, I want that for my educator friends. I want us each to remember that the successes and failures of the educators who have gone before us, the hard research studies undertaken, and the seminal understandings gained pave the way for us. Many scholars have shown us the way over the years, with the goal of ensuring that we use these bodies of knowledge and understanding to provide the best for our students.

2. **I will remember that there is art to medicine as well as science, and that warmth, sympathy, and understanding may outweigh the surgeon's knife or the chemist's drug.**

While medicine is largely clinical (the science), there is an art to it that includes listening, considering, and understanding. Realizing there is an art to teaching creates the possibility of joy and passion, along with challenge and precision. It is the art, when matched with the science in education, that ensures that students are considered first. It ensures that families and caregivers are seen as partners and that the classroom is a dynamic place for all.

3. I will not be ashamed to say, "I know not," nor will I fail to call in my colleagues when the skills of another are needed for a patient's recovery.

It is my hope that a doctor, when stymied by a condition or illness, will be open to the support of a colleague, optimally one who has researched the condition or has a deeper understanding based on experience. Educators, too, should strive for the candor of asking for help and for the willingness to listen. As professionals, each time we open a professional resource, read a research article, or engage in professional learning, we are acknowledging that there is more to know.

In essence, the oath speaks to us, as educators. We can align our professionalism to that of medical professionals. We, too, consistently promise to "do no harm." We create classrooms filled with joy and learning, love and laughter, and rigor and challenge. While there is no formal oath for teachers, each day upon beginning class, we promise to listen to the wisdom of the research, to remember the art and science of the work we do, and to be unafraid of requesting help when needed. We are dedicated.

It is not always easy. Sometimes, the research is complex, confusing, or seems contradictory. Education can be a whirlwind. Standards change. Curriculum changes. Expectations change. Legislation changes. And lately, these changes are compounded by added pressures. But the need for young people to develop literacy skills does not waver. Reading, writing, speaking, and listening consistently reign as must-have skills.

Several years ago, I stood on a stage in front of eager educators, ready to begin the new year. We were talking about literacy, engaged in the conversation around the importance of reading challenging texts. Education was in the midst of change, and for many, it was an intense, scary change. The research (what we now call "the science") was indicating the need for systemic change. We needed then, as educators need now, to be ready, willing, and able to heed the research and orchestrate instructional change within our classrooms. The purpose of this book is to support that goal.

What Is the Science of Reading?

This book is one in a series of professional resources that provides a close look at the discussion around the Science of Reading (SOR). What exactly does that mean? The term *the Science of Reading* pervades the national conversation around the best literacy instruction for all students. The purpose of this series is to close the gap between the knowledge and understanding of what

> We create classrooms filled with joy and learning, love and laughter, and rigor and challenge.

students need to become literate humans and the instructional practices in our schools. This gap is widely acknowledged yet remains largely intact. While research is available, journals are not easy to navigate. "It would be the proverbial needle in a haystack problem trying to find the most relevant information" (Kilpatrick 2015, 6). With concise resources that build understanding of the body of research, however, teachers can be equipped with the logical steps to find success. Mark Seidenberg notes, "A look at the basic science suggests specific ways to promote reading success" (2017, 9).

The great news is that this book will help you navigate the important research that informs the Science of Reading conversations. Let's begin by quickly breaking down the words behind the hype: the *Science* of *Reading*.

> **Science:** a branch of knowledge or study dealing with a body of facts or truths systematically arranged and showing the operation of general laws *or* systematic knowledge of the physical or material world gained through observation and experimentation
>
> **Read[ing]:** looking at carefully so as to understand the meaning of (something written, printed, etc.) (dictionary.com 2022)

Bottom line? The Science of Reading is the collection of excellent research that leads to the understanding of how students learn to read. What are the best ways to support students as they break down the code of the English language? How can teachers provide the best instruction for developing fluency? What are the structures within text and embedded within instruction that will best support students as they decipher text and develop the skills to understand a range of genres in various contexts and content areas? Which strategies will best help students develop the ability to write with adequate voice, grammatical control, and knowledge? The answers are found in the collection of research, studies, and experiences (the ultimate educators of the universe) known as the Science of Reading. Many of the research studies have been duplicated, reinforcing the understanding of how students learn to read.

To be clear, nothing about this body of work is brand new. There are ebbs and flows within any conversation, and while some of the conversations around the SOR have resurfaced in recent times with great enthusiasm and debate, the basic components of this body of research have been discussed among literacy researchers and educators for many years.

Figure I.1—Components of Literacy

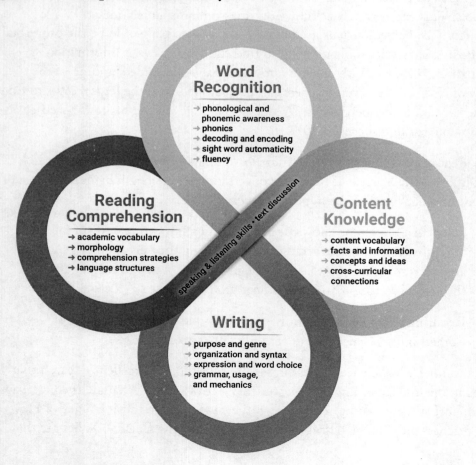

Figure I.1 demonstrates an approach to linking the research-based components of the Science of Reading, highlighting word recognition, reading comprehension, content knowledge, and writing. A very intentional decision has been made to include the science of *literacies*, including reading and writing as well as recognizing the power of speaking and listening, in this series. Each book will explore instructional implications, best practices, and things to look for in classrooms, as well as identify educational practices to reconsider. (To best incorporate pedagogical practices, reading comprehension and content knowledge are presented in one book.) These books were developed to support professional growth, enhance engagement, and provide support in designing instruction that uses the best research-based strategies.

This research base and understanding are integral to instruction in today's classrooms. Yet, despite a general knowledge of these ideas, many students continue to be plagued by inadequate literacy skills. Pulling from the work of educators, psychologists, neurologists, special educators, and more, our hope is that a renewed focus on the science ("body of facts or truths") of literacy will support a change in instructional practices and lead to higher literacy achievement.

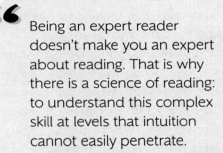

> Being an expert reader doesn't make you an expert about reading. That is why there is a science of reading: to understand this complex skill at levels that intuition cannot easily penetrate.
> —Mark Seidenberg (2017, 4)

Seminal Works to Build Understanding

Foundational works set the tone for understanding how research illuminates the pathway for instruction within the classroom. These seminal, theoretical pieces of research are widely recognized and serve as the guides to the books in this series. We will begin the journey with research and theories from the mid-1980s. Philip B. Gough and William E. Tunmer's seminal model of how young people learn to read, the Simple View of Reading (SVR), builds our understanding in a simple and usable manner. This widely used model has been manipulated to support new models since its origination. The Simple View of Reading (figure I.2) articulates the basic components of how people become comprehenders of text.

Figure I.2—Simple View of Reading

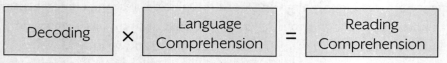

Research indicating that reading comprehension is the product of decoding (word-level reading) and language comprehension is showcased in an equation that defines the skills needed to become a reader (Gough and Tunmer 1986). The idea presented by the SVR is that strong reading comprehension depends on both decoding and language comprehension being present and strong. When one component is absent, reading comprehension will not occur. Although they are depicted simply in figure I.2, the skill domains of decoding and language comprehension include complex constructs that need to be understood separately and in relation to other constructs. *Decoding* (word-level reading) includes print concepts, phonological awareness, phonics and word recognition, and word knowledge. *Language comprehension* includes background knowledge, academic language, academic vocabulary, inferential language skills, and narrative language skills. Intentionally represented as multiplicative rather than additive, the Simple View of Reading highlights that reading comprehension is a result of both successful decoding and comprehension.

In 2001, Hollis Scarborough expanded on the foundation of the SVR in an effort to better support parents in understanding how children acquire the skills to be successful readers. Her Reading Rope (figure I.3) shows how the skills of word recognition and language comprehension come together to support proficient reading. Not only are the many components of decoding and language comprehension interrelated, the two skill areas must be integrated for reading comprehension to take place.

The lower strands of the rope represent *word recognition*, weaving together phonological awareness (awareness of sounds within words), decoding (an understanding that sounds are encoded and decoded by the alphabet), and sight recognition (automaticity with frequently used words). These strands braid together as the portion of the rope that ensures students can pull print from texts.

The upper strands of the rope signify *language comprehension*. These include background and content knowledge, vocabulary, language structures, verbal reasoning, and literacy knowledge. These strands articulate the range of comprehension skills, strategies, and knowledge that support reading with fluency and understanding.

Figure I.3—Scarborough's Reading Rope

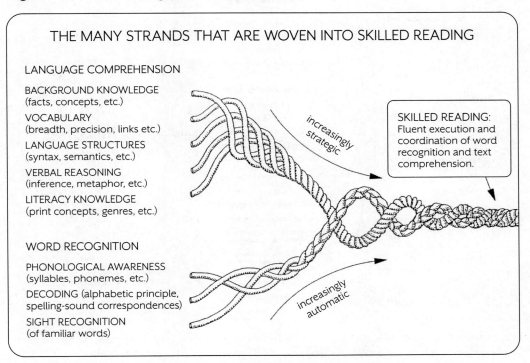

THE MANY STRANDS THAT ARE WOVEN INTO SKILLED READING

LANGUAGE COMPREHENSION

BACKGROUND KNOWLEDGE
(facts, concepts, etc.)
VOCABULARY
(breadth, precision, links etc.)
LANGUAGE STRUCTURES
(syntax, semantics, etc.)
VERBAL REASONING
(inference, metaphor, etc.)
LITERACY KNOWLEDGE
(print concepts, genres, etc.)

WORD RECOGNITION

PHONOLOGICAL AWARENESS
(syllables, phonemes, etc.)
DECODING (alphabetic principle,
spelling-sound correspondences)
SIGHT RECOGNITION
(of familiar words)

increasingly strategic

increasingly automatic

SKILLED READING:
Fluent execution and coordination of word recognition and text comprehension.

Credit: Hollis Scarborough, "Connecting Early Language and Literacy to Later Reading (Dis)abilities: Evidence, Theory, and Practice" in *Handbook of Research in Early Literacy*, edited by Susan B. Neuman and David K. Dickinson © Guilford Press, 2001. Used with permission.

Researchers have continued to develop and articulate models of how reading works. In 2021, Duke and Cartwright introduced the Active View of Reading (figure I.4), a powerful model that extends the understandings from both the Simple View of Reading and Scarborough's Reading Rope. The Active View of Reading model recognizes the intersection between word recognition and language comprehension, referring to this intersection as the *bridging processes*. These processes are a departure from previous models, as they articulate the relationship and authentic merging of word recognition and language comprehension. The Active View of Reading also includes active self-regulation, which impacts word recognition, bridging processes, and language comprehension. Active self-regulation includes motivation and engagement, as well as executive function skills and the use of strategies.

Figure I.4—Duke and Cartwright's Active View of Reading

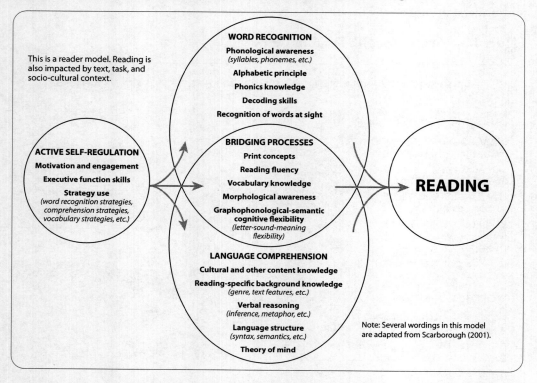

Credit: Nell K. Duke and Kelly B. Cartwright, "The Science of Reading Progresses: Communicating Advances Beyond the Simple View of Reading." *Reading Research Quarterly*, Vol. 56: Issue SI. © 2021 The Authors. Used with permission.

Each of these theoretical frameworks helps educators understand the essential components that need to be part of instruction as students learn to read. Moving beyond these frameworks, a nuanced understanding of how the brain navigates print to master the reading process supports effective instruction. Numerous researchers have written about the phases of predictable reading development (Ehri 1995, Ehri and McCormick 1998, and Ehri and Snowling 2004). These phases, supported by instruction, provide readers with the ability to recognize words "by sight." The phases include the following:

- **Prealphabetic reading:** Reader uses a range of visual clues, such as a picture or a logo, to "read" words. Reader does not yet understand the letter-sound relationship.

- **Partial alphabetic reading and writing:** Reader uses some grapheme-phoneme, or letter-sound, connections. This is known as *phonetic cue reading*. At this stage, the connections are not fully reliable.

- **Full alphabetic reading and writing:** Reader has basic sound/symbol correspondences and attends to every letter in every word. At this stage, readers can convert letters into sounds and words.

- **Consolidated alphabetic reading:** Reader has some sight vocabulary and a breadth of strategies to read unknown words. Reader uses chunks of words to support the reading of words.

- **Automatic reading:** Reader is skilled and recognizes most words. Unfamiliar words are approached with a variety of strategies.

Orthographic Mapping

Another term for how words are retrieved is *orthographic mapping*. According to David Kilpatrick, "Orthographic mapping is the process readers use to store written words for immediate, effortless retrieval. It is the means by which readers turn unfamiliar words into familiar, instantaneously accessible sight words" (2015, 81). In orthographic mapping, readers use the oral language processing part of their brains to match phonemes (sounds within words) to the letters found inside words. As this mapping becomes more fluent, readers can instantly recognize words.

Five Essential Components

Research continues in the field of education. In 2000, the National Reading Panel (NRP) published its review of studies to identify the components of effective reading instruction. This comprehensive report carefully examined a wide range of research. Within its narrative about how readers develop, the NRP's report articulated five essential components of reading:

- **Phonemic Awareness:** manipulating individual speech sounds
- **Phonics:** matching sounds to letters for use in reading and spelling
- **Fluency:** reading connected text accurately and fluently
- **Vocabulary:** knowing the meanings of words in speech and print
- **Reading Comprehension:** understanding what is read

Since the report was published, further research has only added to the body of research that supports the findings. The bottom line? Research continues to highlight the importance of integrated approaches to literacy instruction that include the five essential components in an intertwined way. Ultimately, the best ways to ensure students become engaged and successful readers and writers have not changed significantly.

This foundational information lays the groundwork for continued understanding of how to engage students with solid literacy instruction. Several institutions provide briefs or guides that present research in easily digestible formats. The Institute of Educational Sciences/What Works Clearinghouse Practice Guides provide educators with sound instructional practices related to a range of literacy skills. Additionally, the International Literacy Association provides Leadership Briefs that highlight integral pedagogy with a strong research base.

The Focus on Comprehension

Much of the above discussion about the Science of Reading highlighted the importance of foundational skills. When students do not have the language and strategies to navigate the meaning of text, their reading brains can only partially develop. The Simple View of Reading (Gough and Tunmer 1986) articulates the equal importance of word recognition and language comprehension to achieve reading comprehension, while the Active View of Reading (Duke and Cartwright 2021) identifies additional factors in successful comprehension. These include active self-regulation and the bridging processes between word recognition and comprehension. Certainly, the purpose of engaging with text is to understand it. Hence, the focus, ultimately, on reading comprehension. A delineation of the range of skills, strategies, and understandings needed for comprehension is complex, yet essential for developing skilled readers. Recall the strands of Scarborough's Reading Rope that wind together with increasing capability (2001). These components encompass the nuances of language that impact how individuals understand what they read.

Whichever model an educator uses to teach reading, ensuring students develop language knowledge and understanding to navigate text is multifaceted. Douglas Fisher, Nancy Frey, and John Hattie explain, "[It] is achieved through the use of a host of instructional practices designed to equip students with the ability to organize and analyze knowledge; link it to information about the social, biological, and physical worlds; reflect upon it; and take action" (2016, 56). In considering the language comprehension portion of the reading models, students must have both the understanding of the structures of the language and the knowledge and vocabulary needed to connect them together.

Much happens within the brain when a person engages with text. This can be illustrated by our own experiences. We have all been faced with a piece of text with words we were able to read, yet we were unable to make sense of what we had read. For Jen, that happened recently when examining a textbook at high school orientation for her youngest child. Decoding, no problem. Sentence structure, success. However, she was stumped by the vocabulary. She was missing the knowledge to connect with what she was reading and make sense of it.

In the classroom, teachers can support the development of language comprehension by considering how to strategically develop the parts of it that impact overall reading comprehension. This instruction is an imperative component for all students.

A Bit about Text: Building Knowledge and Vocabulary

Later in this section, you will have the joy of reading about a second grader who was deeply immersed in learning about plants. Learning about plants is interesting, fun, important—not because the vocabulary that describes plants in detail is of the greatest significance, but rather because this vocabulary has utility and context that is transferable. Understanding plant life cycles supports students in making connections and understanding animal life cycles. Determining the needs for successful plant growth can aid students as they develop understandings about survival needs. Familiarity with different kinds of vegetation likely will support students as they read complex details that describe settings in pieces of literature. The more students know, the more they can relate to new information, further building their knowledge. Vocabulary and background knowledge influence comprehension (Stahl et al. 1991). One powerful consideration in choosing texts is how they can be used to intentionally develop knowledge and vocabulary. Exposure to a wide range of complex texts increases students' access to both of those things. Text sets or collections can be created to support this development, so students read multiple, varying texts about the same topic.

A Bit about Text: Complexity

Complexity is another important consideration when selecting texts. Determining text complexity is multifaceted and worthy of understanding. All students deserve access to rich, powerful, interesting text that is complex and that builds their knowledge and vocabulary. Ensuring equity in the text students have regular access to is an integral component of its selection. Using the range of complexity measures outlined in figure I.5, teachers can select text that is appropriately complex to build students' reading brains.

Figure I.5—Complexity Measures and Considerations

Complexity Measure	Considerations
Qualitative Measures of Text	• Level of meaning and clarity of purpose • Structure of language • Knowledge demands placed on reader
Quantitative Measures of Text	• Length of words and sentences • Frequency of unfamiliar words • Lexile® level or grade-level equivalent of the text
Reader and **Task**	• Background knowledge needed • Reader's independent reading level • Reader's next steps

Settled Science

When considering the body of research that is now known as the Science of Reading, there are implications for instruction that can be considered settled. David Kilpatrick (2015) notes, "We teach reading in different ways; [students] learn to read proficiently in only one way" (39). Recognizing that certain pedagogies and practices are settled science allows all educators to infuse them in their instruction. Instruction must be:

> Reading levels should not be about denying access; they should be understood mostly as indications of what it takes to grant access to complex, grade-level text.
> —Cindy Jiban (2020, para. 5)

Evidence-based: Instruction and materials are anchored in trustworthy and reliable evidence. The evidence should indicate a consistent success record in increasing students' literacy abilities. Practices should build skills in phonemic awareness, phonics, vocabulary development, reading fluency (including oral-language skills), and reading comprehension.

Explicit: Instruction should include direct teaching that provides explanations of the concepts, modeling of the concepts, and practice with the concepts. Instruction should be clear, specific, and directly connected to an objective.

Systematic: Instruction should follow thoughtfully planned instructional routines. These routines should be planned in advance, ensuring maximum time on task.

Sequential: Instruction should teach skills and concepts sequentially from easiest to hardest. Foundational skills are taught to support higher-order skills. Sequencing should be intentional and implemented within and across grades.

Rigorous for all: Instruction must include complex texts and tasks for all students. Referring to the practice of having students read only books at "their level," Sue Pimentel notes, "The texts they're reading don't require them to decipher unfamiliar vocabulary, confront challenging concepts, or parse new and complicated language" (2018, para. 5). Every student needs opportunities to engage with difficult vocabulary, to build their knowledge and strengthen their skills.

> "It is called *explicit* because it is an unambiguous and direct approach to teaching that includes both instructional design and delivery procedures.
>
> —Anita Archer (2011, 1)"

Intentional: Instruction should thoughtfully align to grade-level standards, and it should be scaffolded to support student needs. Assessment provides an understanding of what students know and what they need to know.

Engaging: Instruction should ensure students have clear understanding of the objectives. It should enable students to make connections to their out-of-school lives and see the relevance of the work. Instruction should provide students with challenges and opportunities to take risks (Jackson and Zmuda 2014).

Designed to build knowledge: Instruction should be designed to build knowledge, vocabulary, and understanding about a range of topics. In a brief for the Knowledge Matters Campaign, Daniel Willingham notes, "Students need deep knowledge of a subject in order to think creatively or critically about it" (2016, 1).

Aligned to the essential components: Instruction must match what the evidence indicates is integral for literacy instruction. Instruction should focus on the five essential components showcased by the NRP (see page 15). Written expression (composition) and oral language (speaking and listening) are also essential components of literacy.

From the Classroom

There was a buzz in the air. Excitement had taken over the 23 second graders at Fisher Elementary School. Each student was carefully holding a magnifying glass up to their blossoming bean inside a plastic bag. I heard chatter. The stir was serious. Finally, I asked, "What is happening? What are you observing?" It was Brenton who responded. He was proud, convincing. "Germination!" he exclaimed. Soon, the students had found their science journals and had begun recording their observations. Pencils were forming the words *sprout, germinate, roots,* and *damp.*

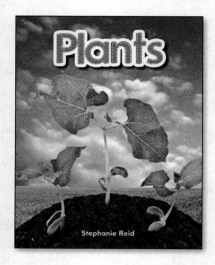

These vocabulary words were among those that students had discovered through a range of language opportunities over several weeks. Students had engaged with several texts introducing them to plant life cycles and what plants need to survive. They had access to a brochure from a local greenhouse. Several short video clips had been shown to them, with anticipatory guides and graphic organizers to support their learning.

The class had continued their learning—planting brassica seeds, reading, writing, and discussing. We had dissected the texts, learning about how authors used text features to help navigate information. Students had discovered places where authors supported the understanding of difficult language and how the structure of sentences could be used to help figure it out. Students had built knowledge and understanding about how language works within text *and* about plants.

I do not have to wonder how Brenton knew the relevant vocabulary word, *germination.*

Navigating This Book

Each of the first six chapters of this book showcases important research that supports the instruction of reading comprehension in the classroom. This includes literacy, mathematics, science, and social studies classrooms.

Chapter 1	Building Content Knowledge
Chapter 2	All about Vocabulary
Chapter 3	Literacy Knowledge: Print Concepts to Genre Study
Chapter 4	Language Structures: Syntax and Semantics
Chapter 5	Text Structures and Verbal Reasoning
Chapter 6	Reading Comprehension Strategies

These chapters are structured to bridge the gap between the science of literacy instruction and classroom practice. Each chapter begins by examining the research with a thoughtful and critical eye. Following the research, you will find instructional implications. These implications identify how the research should impact the work of educators in classrooms today. Next, you will find key terms for teacher understanding. Each of these terms is defined and showcased in a classroom example.

Each chapter also includes research-based instructional strategies. These strategies are aligned to grade-level bands: K–1, 2–3, 4–5, and secondary. However, many of these strategies have utility across grade levels and can be modified to support students beyond the bands suggested. Each chapter closes with the following sections:

- **Top Must-Dos:** A summary of research implications, the must-do list supports all teachers as they navigate taking the science of reading directly into their classrooms.

- **Further Considerations:** Offering additional insights about effective instruction, this section also includes (as appropriate) guidance for moving away from practices that are not supported by research.

- **Reflection Questions:** A short list of questions to use as conversation starters for professional learning or for self-reflection.

The final chapter in this book, written by guest author Carrie Eicher, explores the importance of culturally responsive texts in literacy instruction to help students make connections between what they read and what they already know, and to think deeply about what they have read. She examines the power of using such texts to open up new understandings and possibilities for students.

Take a deep breath. While we educators do not have a Hippocratic oath, we know the great responsibility we face each day. Louisa Moats (2020) said it best: "Teaching reading *is* rocket science" (para. 7). Let's build the literacy rocket together.

Chapter 1

Building Content Knowledge

From the Classroom

During a fourth-grade lesson related to landforms, the teacher defines a lake as a body of water surrounded by land. She then asks the class, "What are the names of some lakes?" No hands go up. She asks again, "There's a lake just one mile from school. What's the name of that lake?" Again, no students raise their hands. After pulling down a map of the United States, she points and asks, "What is the name of one of the Great Lakes?" No response. Continuing to prompt the students, the teacher asks, "Has anyone been to see the fireworks at Jackson Park?" Now, students get excited. At least half of them had been to see the fireworks on Lake Jackson. Once the connection is made, students are able to name Lake Jackson as a body of water that fits the definition they were given.

These students knew what a lake was. They would know one if they saw one. However, when faced with the challenge of connecting their knowledge with the vocabulary and naming lakes, the group struggled. They were left unsure of what to share. As soon as the teacher provided logical, relevant context, students made connections. When their knowledge was illuminated, they could name one lake.

Background Information and Research

Background knowledge is exactly what it sounds like: knowledge of facts and concepts about a topic, problem, or situation students have when engaging with instructional content. In fact, before beginning this chapter, you, the reader, have already skillfully accessed your background knowledge in preparation for how you will interact with this text.

Teachers likely consider background knowledge to be facts and information students have that they can use to comprehend content-area informational text. However, background knowledge is more than just facts. It is a composite of all the experiences, vocabulary, and personal interests and interactions students have ever had. Background knowledge and understanding impact how students engage with and understand text. Thus, one significant priority in developing students who comprehend text is ensuring that students have adequate knowledge and understanding to support them as they learn and engage with new content. Students have a working and growing knowledge base. For students to build knowledge, they must have regular access to rich and captivating informational text and stories.

> For students to build knowledge, they must have regular access to rich and captivating informational text and stories.

Importantly, students will attain more information and build more background when their learning is structured to introduce and explore specific topics and ideas. For example, second graders can dig into learning about plants: they can engage with informational books about plants, articles about plants, and a story that takes place in a rooftop garden, as well as pictures and short video clips that discuss plant life cycles. This approach supports the building of knowledge and allows students to develop a robust understanding of a topic that is fundamental and supports learning across contexts.

Connection to the Rope

Background knowledge is one of the pieces of the Language Comprehension strand of Scarborough's Reading Rope (2001). The Language Comprehension strand articulates the notion that all new learning builds on prior learning (Wexler 2019). Students must have or build sufficient knowledge if they are to understand a situation or problem, text or activity. Students use knowledge to engage with text and understand what they read. As students gain new knowledge, they add it to their existing background knowledge to support continued understanding. When this knowledge building is done with intention, the cycle continues and supports students with more complex texts and tasks. As students learn, their knowledge grows. As their knowledge grows, they can build new connections and learn more. Informational text becomes more comprehensible. Narrative text, too, will be experienced with greater comfort and understanding.

Reid Smith et al. (2021) conducted a critical review of the influence of background knowledge on reading comprehension. The review examined how background knowledge of primary school–age children affected their reading comprehension and the implications that has for instruction. They discovered that "higher levels of background knowledge have a range of effects that are influenced by the nature of the text, the quality of the situation model required, and the presence of reader misconceptions about the text" (para. 1). The study recognized that students' reading skills also factor into how well they can build background knowledge.

Based on the review, Smith et al. "consistently found that higher levels of background knowledge enable children to better comprehend a text" (para. 32). They also discovered that students with limited background knowledge could succeed with recall and summarizing tasks since these did not require students to integrate their own knowledge to demonstrate comprehension. Conversely, students with strong background knowledge and limited reading skills could compensate for their lack of reading skills and demonstrate comprehension.

When reviewing how student misconceptions (inaccurate background knowledge) impacted comprehension, Smith et al. found that highly skilled readers would "identify contradictions between prior knowledge and information in the text." However, readers who had not developed strong skills would rely on their incorrect background knowledge more so than the new, correct information they read about.

> As students gain new knowledge, they add it to their existing background knowledge to support continued understanding.

Additionally, M. A. K. Halliday and Ruqaiya Hassan (2014) identified two key factors that impact students' ability to comprehend text based on background knowledge. They are the **cohesion** and **coherence** of the text. Texts with high cohesion make direct connections between concepts and ideas and between sentences and paragraphs. Texts with high coherence provide students with information and cues to relate information across different parts of the text. Texts with low cohesion and coherence require readers to rely on background knowledge to comprehend the information. Students do not need to rely as heavily on background knowledge when reading texts with high cohesion and coherence.

Implications for Teaching and Learning

Teachers know that every student arrives at school with a unique and wide variety of background knowledge. Background knowledge is connected to students' lives, schools, and cultural experiences. For example, students who live in rural settings tend to have different life experiences, and therefore background knowledge, than students living in suburban and urban areas. These differences create unique challenges for teachers. One of the most powerful opportunities we can provide to students is a well-rounded base of knowledge to build upon. While educators have little opportunity to influence the learning that students bring to school, there is an enormous opportunity for educators to build knowledge through thoughtfully planned opportunities to engage with quality content that is worthy of knowing and developmentally appropriate. Because background knowledge is essential for reading comprehension, teachers must provide adequate experiences and information to students prior to embarking on a new topic or concept. This intentional knowledge-building endeavor provides students with the connectors they need to be successful with new text.

> When teachers begin by both activating knowledge and identifying any potential misinformation, they open the door for learning that will create a body of knowledge to continue to build upon.

Before reading any text, teachers can and should first **activate** students' background knowledge. Jeffrey Wilhelm, Adam Fachler, and Rachel Bear, the authors of *Planning Powerful Instruction* (2019), explain, "This process honors what students bring to the classroom and provides them with necessary context and connection to the purpose and payoff of what is to be learned" (as quoted in Ferlazzo 2020, para. 8).

As students engage in new learning, teachers should prime them by activating background knowledge in a variety of ways. Posing a simple question such as, "What do you know about our solar system?" will lead to an array of answers. Providing the opportunity to engage with background knowledge will support students as they engage with new text. In these anticipatory activities, teachers may discover gaps in understanding or misconceptions. Did some students not recognize the sun as a star or Earth as a planet? Are students confused about the difference between rotation and revolution? Will misconceptions and understandings be supported through the reading, or do students need further information to find success within the text? When teachers begin by both activating knowledge and identifying any potential misinformation, they open the door for learning that will create a body of knowledge to continue to build upon.

Since we cannot (yet) jump into a starship and launch ourselves into space to experience these ideas firsthand, we must provide students with meaningful and purposeful learning experiences to build this background knowledge so that students may learn new, accurate facts about the solar system. This allows students to access even more content by seeing "the connection between previous and current learning" (Wilhelm, Fachler, and Bear quoted in Ferlazzo 2020, para. 11). In addition to posing introductory questions, teachers build content knowledge by watching videos, accessing relevant websites, providing hands-on activities, conducting real-life or online simulations, providing images of complex concepts, and explicitly teaching essential vocabulary.

Common Practices

Two powerful strategies for building reading are the **read-aloud** and **shared reading**. "Decades of research highlight the instructional benefits of read-alouds" (International Literacy Association 2018). To conduct a read-aloud, the teacher selects a text—a story, an article, or another piece—to build knowledge and vocabulary to support learning for a specific topic. The teacher reads the text aloud to students. During a shared reading, the teacher provides additional opportunities for students to engage with the text as it is read aloud. When selecting texts for read-aloud or shared reading, challenging and rigorous texts provide opportunities to expose students to vocabulary and knowledge about a topic. While students may not be able to access the text independently, the shared experience provides them with extensive opportunities to engage with the rich content, vocabulary, and knowledge. Since students are listening and not decoding, they only need to focus on making sense of the story or information.

> By first activating, then building background knowledge with meaningful and purposeful activities and experiences, teachers provide students with the information they need to be more successful with content-area reading.

When activating and building background knowledge for students, teachers should consider how the activities, experiences, and interactions they use impact learning. In a study of rural students, Courtney Hattan (2019) discovered "that not all prior knowledge activation techniques are equally effective for all students" (454). One common activation strategy is the K-W-L, or Know, Want to Know, Learned chart. This was originally presented by Donna Ogle in 1986, and it is still widely used in classrooms today. However, Hattan discovered that the utility of the K-W-L chart experience and its outcomes are distinctly impacted by how much students knew about the topic to begin with. In comparing this activation strategy to in-text strategy work, students fared better when they engaged more while reading. Hattan speculated, "One possible explanation is that students had fairly low topic-specific prior knowledge. Therefore, [K-W-L] students did not have sufficient topic knowledge to draw on, whereas the text annotation students focused their attention on the specific details presented in the text and were then able to demonstrate recollection of that information in the topic knowledge post-assessment" (454).

Another of Hattan's findings was that having students use **relational reasoning** (RR) to derive patterns among content "proved highly effective for promoting students' comprehension. RR allowed students to make connections not only to prior topic knowledge but also to other sources of relevant knowledge" (454). The RR strategy supported both high- and low-achieving students.

With relational reasoning, students recognize similarities and differences between their personal background knowledge and new information. Consider the previous example of learning about the solar system: students may reflect that they thought a year was one rotation of Earth, when it is actually one revolution around the sun. Hattan notes, "These relational patterns may be particularly beneficial for students when answering higher-level comprehension questions or those that require deep text processing or critique and evaluation of the content" (452–453).

At the beginning of this chapter, you, the reader, considered your own understanding of building knowledge. Hopefully, you now have a greater knowledge base about the research that supports building knowledge. The research shows several points:

- Knowledge is important when students engage with informational text about a new topic or concept.
- Building knowledge works in tandem with the text.
- Students with limited background knowledge can still read and comprehend informational text when it is cohesive and coherent.
- Making connections between what students know and what they are reading helps them better learn and understand the content.

Building knowledge is important. Providing opportunities for students to strategically build knowledge through carefully selected texts and activities will aid students' learning. It is equally important to ensure that students have strategies to be able to fuse new and old information. Gina N. Cervetti and Elfrieda H. Hiebert (2018) describe three ways teachers may help students integrate background knowledge with information in text. To connect new and prior knowledge, teachers can use higher-level questions. This allows students to bridge the gap between what they know and what they are learning. For example, if students are learning about animal coverings, they may learn about shells, feathers, fur, and scales. Inferential questions such as *Which animal covering do you think is the best for warmth? Protection? Hiding from predators?* engage students in thinking and connecting pieces of information. There are often multiple correct answers or ideas in response to these questions. Students must use both their background knowledge and facts and evidence from the text to back up their responses. This level of questioning organically supports students as they navigate new information.

> " The formation of connections helps us to construct richer meaning than just describing what we see or describing the literal events of a text.
> —Gina N. Cervetti and Elfrieda H. Hiebert (2018, 14) "

Second, Cervetti and Hiebert suggest teachers provide explicit instruction on how to make different kinds of connections in text. When learning about animal coverings, teachers should model connections to prior knowledge ("I knew tortoises had hard coverings called shells"), prior texts ("I remember from Monday's reading that armadillos and turtles also have shells"), and information within text ("I understand that shells offer protection from predators because they are hard"). These statements are directly related to the text, not necessarily to students' own experiences with the topic. Students may have seen armadillos, turtles, and tortoises, but this background knowledge is not directly related to the information students are reading about—specifically, how shells provide protection.

Finally, Cervetti and Hiebert suggest "a range of media, including texts, objects, images, and cartoons can be used for practice in inferring" (2018, 13). For example, students may look at pictures of different types of armadillos, turtles, and tortoises to compare their shells, noting similarities and differences among the wide variety of creatures. Teachers can then connect this information to have students (in the words of the third-grade standard) "use evidence to construct an explanation for how the variations in characteristics among individuals

> From an educator's perspective, surface learning involves recalling and reproducing content and skills. Deep learning involves things like extending ideas, detecting patterns, applying knowledge and skills in new contexts or in creative ways, and being critical of arguments and evidence.
>
> —Merrilyn Goos
> (University of Queensland 2017)

of the same species may provide advantages in surviving, finding mates, and reproducing" (NGSS Lead States 2013). Collectively, "the formation of connections helps us to construct richer meaning than just describing what we see or describing the literal events of a text" (14). This moves students from **superficial knowledge** to **deep knowledge**.

Superficial knowledge, sometimes called *shallow knowledge*, refers to the obvious. Students can learn about a topic, apply learning, and solve problems based on what they know. For example, students may learn that electrical energy can be transformed into light, heat, sound, and mechanical energy. However, when shown a picture of a television, they identify the energy transfer as electrical to mechanical simply because objects are moving on the screen. They do not equate mechanical energy to the actual movement of the object (the television). This requires deep knowledge, sometimes referred to as *profound knowledge*. Having deep knowledge allows students to be able to apply knowledge in novel contexts, not just those they are exposed to in class.

Key Terms for Teacher Understanding

Term and Definition	Example
activate background knowledge—trigger students' knowledge about a topic, using a stimulus	A group of students are learning about Earth and the sun and moon. They will be reading about the moon as a *satellite*. Mr. Pei believes students know what a satellite is, but perhaps do not recognize the moon as one. He asks, "Where do scientists send satellites?" Several students raise their hands, and one reveals that satellites fly above Earth. Mr. Pei clarifies that, yes, satellites do *orbit* Earth. Then, he asks, "What else in the sky orbits Earth?" One student says the sun, and another says the moon. He leaves this question unresolved to clarify during reading.
background knowledge—collective and combined knowledge gained through study, experiences, interactions, and instruction	Carlos and his lab group are using properties of matter to separate a mixture. The directions say to empty the mixture of sand, paper clips, and pebbles into a *sieve*. Neither Carlos nor his lab partners have ever heard of this word before. They ask the teacher what it means. She responds by asking if anyone has ever drained spaghetti in a large pot with holes. Of course! The students now know that a *sieve* has holes that will let the sand fall through, leaving the paper clips and pebbles behind. Next, they will use a magnet to separate the paper clips from the pebbles.
build background knowledge—provide essential prerequisite knowledge to expand on the topic	A first-grade class is learning about rules. They will read a text about how rules keep things fair and people safe. After reading, the teacher makes statements of both fair and unfair and safe and unsafe situations. The students must build on their new understanding of rules to explain why each situation is or isn't fair or safe.

Term and Definition	Example
deep knowledge—integration of previous knowledge with new knowledge to understand underlying principles	Mr. Enberg's history students are comparing government systems. After reading about them, students read different situations and identify which type of government systems they apply to.
read-aloud—a text the teacher reads to students, modeling aloud how to read with purpose and meaning	Mrs. King reads *I Am a Capybara* by Michela Fabbri (2020) to her third-grade students as they begin a new unit on classifying animals. While she reads, Mrs. King pauses to think about how a capybara compares to other animals mentioned in the story. She models the use of "I wonder" questions and "I notice" statements at appropriate points in the text.
relational reasoning—an executive function that supports ability to see meaningful patterns in information	Fourth graders examine a set of words, discern their meanings, and use relational reasoning to sort the words into meaning-based categories.
shared reading—an interactive reading experience shared between the teacher and students	Ms. Melé teaches civics and government to eighth-grade students. She uses a text card titled, "Step Back in Time" from the Smithsonian Institution (n.d.) to support student background knowledge of the suffrage movement. Before reading, she defines *suffrage*, and the class discusses what they know about how past voting rights compare to today's voting rights. She introduces the text, and she and the students take turns reading, pausing to clarify information and then discuss challenges that impede changes to laws.
superficial knowledge—information that is obvious	Second graders read about different types of soil. Then, they match note cards with the descriptions to each type.

Term and Definition	Example
text cohesion—elements in the text are structurally tied together **text coherence**—the unity of ideas within text	In the example below, the topic sentence explains the wonders of the internet. The signal word, *however*, indicates a change in the message. Each "do" idea relates to a "don't" idea. The internet can be a wondrous place. You can meet new people, play online games, and find out about all kinds of things! However, take care when online. NEVER: Share personal information. Reply to people you do not know. Post or share pictures. Click links you are unsure of. Agree to meet someone in person. INSTEAD: Make up a fun screen name. Delete messages from unknown people. Ask a parent to share pictures with your friends and family. Close tabs to questionable websites. Tell an adult about a person who has asked to meet you.

Wonder Wall

Grades: K–1

Description

A Wonder Wall is an excellent way to build and showcase knowledge for students. The teacher creates bulletin board space for an interactive display of student wonderings and subsequent learning. The teacher can use an artifact or picture to jump-start student thinking about a topic, such as *citizenship*. Then, students ask questions and share what they already know to begin building the board. As the class discovers new information, both students and the teacher may add to the Wonder Wall. Primary students can draw and label pictures of their wonderings. The teacher may use sentence strips to post student questions.

Rationale

A Wonder Wall provokes students' curiosity and interest in a topic. It encourages them to be inquisitive and to think more deeply about their learning. And it allows students to creatively express their knowledge. The display captures student learning and understanding. It can also provide teachers with information regarding what students want to learn about, making teaching more personal and allowing students to be more active stakeholders in class. When used during whole-class discussion, it supports essential listening and speaking skills.

Roles and Responsibilities

Teacher: Facilitator

- Labels a bulletin board with the topic.
- Encourages students to ask questions important to them and accepts all ideas.
- Records students' questions and posts them on the bulletin board.
- Follows up by finding answers to students' questions or by weaving in the answers in subsequent lessons.

Student: Thinker

- Thinks about and asks questions related to a topic.
- Takes turns sharing questions.
- Listens to other students' questions and responds to them respectfully.

Process

Introduce a new topic. This can be done verbally or visually. Tell students to think about the topic for 30 seconds to one full minute without talking. During this time, each student should think of at least one question they have about the topic. Records students' questions on sentence strips, or students may draw and label pictures of their wonderings. Help students post their wonderings on the Wonder Wall. Support the discovery and response to students' questions during daily learning about the topic. Allow students to offer additions and responses to the wonderings on the Wonder Wall.

As students gain more knowledge about the topic, encourage them to ask new questions to add to the Wonder Wall. Students may also draw and label pictures to answer questions posted to the Wonder Wall.

Differentiation

If students have difficulty posing questions, remind them of the question words: *who, what, where, when, why,* and *how*. Use sentence frames to support questioning. Model questioning for students. Allow students to work with partners to think of questions to write or draw. Then, partners may share their ideas with the class. Have students working above level free-write for five to ten minutes, then share their ideas with the class.

Word Web

Grades: 2–3

Description

A Word Web is a visual organizer. Students expand the meanings of words or concepts by describing similar words, meanings, or concepts. A Word Web can focus on vocabulary: definitions, synonyms, antonyms, usage, or how the words are used in different contexts. It can also support larger concepts by showing the connections between words.

Rationale

This strategy helps learners acquire and use academic and domain-specific words and phrases. Building a Word Web to introduce students to new ideas supports their understanding of how new terms are related. Students can use Word Webs to make initial connections based on their background knowledge and develop deep understanding of how words interact and relate. When students encounter these words in text, they will have some familiarity with them. This familiarity enables students to fully comprehend the concept.

Roles and Responsibilities

Teacher: Facilitator

- Introduces the Word Web and words.
- Guides discussion to support how the words are organized so students see relationships between and among the words.
- Refers to the Word Web during reading.
- Provides meaningful word-work activities to support student understanding of essential terms.

Student: Active Learner

- Engages with Word Web by repeating, reading, or suggesting words.
- Supports placement of new words into the Word Web throughout learning.
- Completes meaningful activities to understand word definitions.

Process

Create a visual display showing initial words, allowing space for more words so relationships among essential vocabulary terms for a topic can be added to throughout the learning. Introduce core words, asking students to engage with them (read or repeat them). Students may also suggest words. Guide a discussion about how the words are related. Suggested questions include:

- How do these words connect?
- What do these words have in common?
- How are these words different?
- What other words belong here?
- How could we connect these words?

Have students use context clues and visual supports during reading to define the terms and explain what they mean. Throughout learning, add new words and allow students to add new words. Adjust the Word Web and move words as needed to showcase new learning and highlight connections. Provide meaningful activities each day for students to engage with the words.

Research in Action

This example shows a possible third-grade Word Web related to the study of North America. During this unit, students will learn to identify places on a map. Students may have heard these words before, but they likely do not have a context in which to sort or identify them. This Word Web shows the relationship among the different places on the continent. When encountering these terms during reading, students can refer to the web to better conceptualize how they are related.

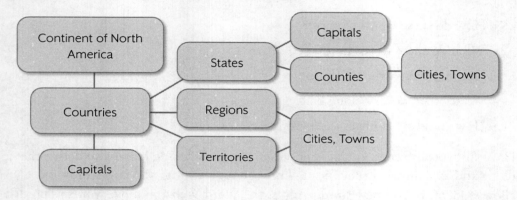

Below are some vocabulary activities to consider using to extend learning.

- The Frayer Model (AdLit, n.d.)—This is a graphic organizer students complete to record the word, list examples and nonexamples, define it, draw a picture of it, and/or list characteristics of it.

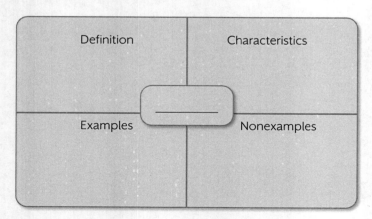

- "Guess My Word"—The teacher or a student gives clues about a word on the Web. Other students use the clues to identify the word.

- Word-Definition Matching Game—The teacher writes the words and their definitions each on their own note cards. Students take turns turning over two cards in an attempt to match the words with their definitions.

Differentiation

Support students by adding hand or body motions or gestures for each term. For example, students may enlarge a "ball" with their arms to model *waxing*, and "deflate the ball" to model *waning*. Provide an outline of the organizer for students to fill in as they are introduced to the words.

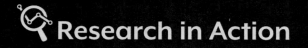

Knowledge Evaluation

Grades: 4–5

Description

This strategy gauges students' familiarity with information before they start learning something new. A Knowledge Evaluation contains statements about the topic, and students rate their familiarity with the information before, during, and after reading. It is useful as a formative assessment during the learning process. And students may use it to identify what they still do not understand after the learning process has concluded. It starts as an anticipation guide, then evolves into a guide for instruction. Students can also use it to review before a summative assessment.

Rationale

Knowledge Evaluations stimulate students' interest in a topic and set a purpose for learning. Students can use them to make predictions, gain insider information as to what they will be reading about, and verify their predictions. Students can use prior knowledge to determine their initial levels of understanding and build curiosity about a new topic. They will learn which ideas they must revisit, and the teacher will know which ideas to review before the summative assessment.

Roles and Responsibilities

Teacher: Statement Generator

- Creates statements about a topic (may be written as "I can" statements).
- Determines students' levels of background knowledge.
- Creates lessons to help students understand the content.
- Provides opportunities to revisit the statements during the learning process.
- Gauges student learning in real time as students adjust their understanding levels.

Student: Self-reflector

- Considers the statements and provides honest responses to indicate level of understanding.
- Revisits the statements throughout the learning process.
- Determines which ideas they need to review or revisit before a summative assessment.

Process

In this example, fifth-grade students are learning about the structure and function of human body systems and organs. Statements related to what students should know and be able to do are on the left. The rating is on the right, beside each idea. Students may use different-color pencils to indicate their understanding as the unit progresses. For example, they may use a red pencil to indicate their familiarity with each system and organ before learning. After they initially learn about each system and organ, they can use a blue pencil to indicate their understanding of each idea. At the conclusion of the unit, students may use a green pencil to indicate how well they have learned each idea. If students do not reach a level 4 or 5, they know they must revisit these ideas, and the teacher will know which ideas to review before the summative assessment.

Ratings:

0—I am not at all familiar with this idea.
1—I have heard this but do not know what it means.
2—I have heard this but cannot explain it.
3—I have heard this, and I can kind of explain it.
4—I have heard this, and I understand what it means.
5—I have heard this, and I can teach others what it means.

Research in Action

Statement	Rating				
I can explain at least two functions of these human body systems:					
digestive	1	2	3	4	5
excretory	1	2	3	4	5
respiratory	1	2	3	4	5
circulatory	1	2	3	4	5
nervous	1	2	3	4	5
muscular and skeletal	1	2	3	4	5
I can explain at least one function of these organs:					
skin	1	2	3	4	5
brain	1	2	3	4	5
heart	1	2	3	4	5
lungs	1	2	3	4	5
stomach	1	2	3	4	5
liver	1	2	3	4	5
intestines	1	2	3	4	5
pancreas	1	2	3	4	5
muscles and skeleton	1	2	3	4	5

Statement	Rating				
kidneys	1	2	3	4	5
bladder	1	2	3	4	5
sensory organs	1	2	3	4	5
I can compare and contrast the function of organs and other physical structures of plants and animals, including humans.	1	2	3	4	5

Differentiation

Read aloud the statements or vocabulary to students. As students continue to learn the concepts, they can discuss each idea with partners and update their familiarity during and after the unit. Provide additional space for students to respond in writing to showcase their learning.

This activity can be adapted for younger students by having them circle or color in a smiley, straight, or frowny face for each statement. Do this before and after learning so students may "see" their learning happening!

Build-up Texts

Secondary Grades

Description

Build-up Texts are short, less complex passages (narrative or informational) that build background for students about complex concepts. They provide situations students may relate to, creating a context for information. They are not a replacement for grade-level, complex text. Instead, they are intended to provide students with background information and exposure to vocabulary.

Rationale

Students in the upper grades read complex text about concepts that may seem nebulous. For example, seventh graders learning about a market economy may struggle to understand the information as they are not bankers or business owners and do not possess the background knowledge to make connections. Using Build-up Texts, teachers provide background knowledge in a context that students will understand. Students will have familiarity with concepts and essential vocabulary. This will help them better understand new information when they encounter ideas in more complex texts about the topic.

Roles and Responsibilities

Teacher: Passage Finder (or Passage Writer)

- Finds or writes a short passage about a topic that students can relate to.
- Leads a discussion about the concepts students will encounter using the Build-up Text as a springboard for discussion.

Student: Reader and Discussion Leader

- Reads the Build-up Text.
- Participates in discussions connecting the passage to the topic.

Process

Remind students of the relatable information when they encounter complex ideas during reading. This short passage introduces seventh-grade students to the ideas of supply and demand, choice, scarcity, and opportunity cost.

> A class wanted to raise money for a field trip by selling fresh fruit. Unfortunately, demand for fresh fruit was low. After one week, the fruit was not fresh anymore, and the class had only sold five items. They lost money the first week. The second week, they tried selling donuts. Their supply of donuts disappeared on the first day! They decided to raise the price by 25 percent. This time, the donuts lasted two and a half days before selling out. But the donuts were still fresh after a couple days, so the customers were happy, and the class was able to raise more money.

After reading the Build-up Text passage, the teacher may guide students to identify examples of each essential term they will encounter when reading complex text about the topic. Providing this background knowledge ahead of time allows students to give meaning to what may otherwise be elusive concepts.

Differentiation

Read aloud the passage to students. Provide time for students to work with partners to predict how the passage relates to the topic. Write the relatable content on a chart, or students may record it in notebooks to reference during instruction. Challenge students to write similar passages during and after instruction. Support students with an infographic, photograph, or other visual that they may refer to when they read complex texts.

Moving Forward: Top Must-Dos

Follow these steps to begin developing lessons that activate and build background knowledge for students.

Identify a Topic and Select Texts to Build Knowledge

Beginning with the underlying knowledge students bring to the table, how they relate to that information, and how they are able to organize it supports their overall success with understanding text. Take time to identify a topic of learning. Review the standards for the subject, and identify pertinent standards that are within the scope and sequence. Use the standards to create student-friendly learning targets or an essential question to guide the learning throughout the unit. Choose a range of related complex texts and engagement activities to support knowledge building.

Determine Text Complexity and Scaffolds Students Will Need

Read the grade-level texts students will encounter during the unit. Consider how the texts explain new information or present new structures, and think about the skills students need to comprehend them. For example, if information is presented in charts, do students have adequate chart-reading skills to understand what the charts show them? Review key vocabulary words. Are the definitions embedded in the texts, or do students need to use context clues to determine what the words mean? Does the story feature a flashback or extensive figurative language? This analysis will help you plan more meaningful and relevant instructional activities that support the challenges within the text.

Identify What Students Need to Know and Do to Be Successful

Determine what students should already know and be able to do to be successful with the reading they will encounter for this topic. Consider the knowledge students bring to the topic. This includes concepts, ideas, vocabulary, and other essential knowledge. Determine a strategy that will activate students' background knowledge and help them begin to engage with the topic and new concepts. Devise ways to help students build background knowledge before and during instruction. This chapter includes four specific strategies to use.

Other suggestions include, but are not limited to, the following:

- brainstorming what students already know about the topic
- making explicit connections between what students already know and new information
- using graphic organizers or other visuals or multimedia resources
- explicitly teaching new vocabulary words
- using multimodal activities that include manipulating objects or ideas, movement, or other sensory experiences
- using anticipation guides

If, while discovering background knowledge, you uncover misconceptions students have about the topic, consider instructional activities and experiences that can help dispel these.

Explicitly draw connections between new concepts or vocabulary terms and the students' background knowledge, understandings, and experiences.

Make note of the strategies and activities that seem to best motivate and engage students in activating their background knowledge. Do these often!

Further Considerations

Remember that background knowledge is one key factor in students' ability to comprehend what they read. However, it is not the only factor. Students with limited background knowledge (and strong reading skills) can read and comprehend facts and information. But if the text itself has too high a readability level, does not make connections for students, or has low coherence and cohesion, they may not be able to comprehend the information. Therefore, teachers may consider providing students with various informational texts below and at students' instructional levels. These texts should connect to a broader purpose for learning information yet be meaningful and relevant to the topic of study.

Further, reconsider the "learning to read/reading to learn" idea. As Laura Robb (2002) reminds us, primary students can read to learn while they learn to read "by practicing and applying reading strategies, as well as by deepening their knowledge of letter and sound relationships, word families, and spelling patterns" (25). In intermediate classrooms, "reading-strategy lessons help students to comprehend, recall, and analyze information in fiction, nonfiction, and content textbooks. At this level, students practice decoding long, multisyllabic words and using clues in the text to understand new words. Learners expand their vocabulary by building words using prefixes, suffixes, and Latin and Greek roots" (25).

Teachers in all grades have students who may struggle with foundational reading skills. Having students apply these in context is not a task only for primary-level teachers. Instead, middle-grade teachers may use scaffolds to support foundational reading skills while simultaneously continuing to build background knowledge. Becton Loveless (n.d.) reports that teachers in upper grades may "mistakenly believe that students have a good grasp on these reading comprehension strategies" (para. 27). He encourages teachers in upper grades to "teach students proven reading comprehension strategies including predicting, questioning, retelling, synthesizing, summarizing, self-monitoring, rereading, close reading, and thinking aloud" (para. 27).

My Teaching Checklist

Are you ready to activate and build students' background knowledge? Use this checklist to help you get started.

Background Knowledge	
Look Fors	**Description**
Knowledge is activated and built through varied instructional approaches.	• Watch videos, access relevant websites, provide hands-on activities, conduct real-life or online simulations, or provide images of complex concepts.
Students are taught carefully selected vocabulary.	• Select vocabulary that supports students' understanding of content. Use varied and proven strategies.
Read-aloud opportunities are provided.	• Use multiple genres that are designed to teach a range of subject areas.
A variety of texts is used.	• Vary complexity, format, and genre. Include a range of text features.

Chapter Summary

Activating and building background knowledge is essential for students to be successful with content-area reading materials. When they make connections with new information, this leads to better understanding and comprehension. Engaging students by asking them to share their knowledge gives them ownership of their learning, validates their backgrounds and experiences, and motivates them to become and stay interested in new learning. Teachers should take time to learn what their students do and don't know so they may provide meaningful background-building experiences to help students be successful with content-area text.

Reflection Questions

1. Why is building background knowledge important? Why is developing a range of knowledge so important?

2. How does students' background knowledge impact their learning?

3. What are some effective ways to build students' background knowledge?

Chapter 2

All about Vocabulary

From the Classroom

Imagine walking into a dark school hallway transformed into a cavern. Students present their projects by acting as tour guides at the Carlsbad Caverns. This type of experience is what you would undergo during a project-based learning demonstration where students solve a real-world challenge. Through this process, students engage with real-world vocabulary they otherwise would not be exposed to.

Students at our school were asked to plan a "field trip" to Carlsbad Caverns, New Mexico, and act as tour guides.

Carlsbad Caverns is about a three-hour drive away, but most of our students have never visited. For this reason, teachers organized a virtual visit with a park ranger and brought in actual brochures from the caverns. This allowed students to be exposed to new experiences and acquire vocabulary. Students were given the opportunity to talk, read, and write about stalagmites, stalactites, limestone, and cave formations. First graders drew pictures labeled with the cavern vocabulary and created their own brochures explaining what could be found when visiting Carlsbad Caverns.

Students further engaged with vocabulary when using cardinal directions to show where the caverns are located. Students created maps showing the midpoint and endpoint of their field trip. Science vocabulary was taught as students developed models of caves to include rocks of different sizes and textures as well as natural sources of water. Vocabulary development was a natural part of this project.

—Christina Castanos
Elementary Science Coordinator
Clint ISD, Texas

Background Information and Research

Out of necessity, when activating and building background knowledge, students rely on their vocabulary. *Vocabulary* is a body of words students use when communicating using language. Students connect some words to their meanings with little effort. For example, when learning about forces and motion, students may readily identify a force as a *push* or *pull* and *gravity* as an example of a force. However, students may struggle to relate other words. They may encounter words they have heard that are not part of their working knowledge, such as *momentum*. Other words, such as *inertia*, may be completely new. Students may never have heard the word. Vocabulary, in all three examples, is important. When learning new content, understanding word meanings supports comprehension. The unfamiliar word *inertia* is part of the definition of Newton's first law of motion. As students are learning this content, they will inevitably need to have some understanding of this term to understand the law. Explicit vocabulary instruction is an integral part of reading comprehension instruction.

Vocabulary is the second component on the Language Comprehension strand of Scarborough's Reading Rope (2001). As students read text, they encounter both familiar and unfamiliar words they must use to make sense of what they are reading. Vocabulary reaches beyond decoding words; students must relate words to ideas or concepts. Understanding the meanings of the words enables students to better comprehend the text.

Tiered Vocabulary

Not all vocabulary that students read has the same impact on their understanding. Generally, educators refer to two categories of vocabulary: academic and domain-specific. Joan Sedita (2016) describes both in her blog. **Academic vocabulary** refers to high-frequency words that appear in multiple subjects but are not usually part of people's everyday conversations. These words may have different meanings depending on the context. They are referred to as *Tier 2 words* by Isabel Beck, Margaret McKeown, and Linda Kucan (2013). Examples of content-area words that appear across subjects include *resource*, *volume*, and *climate*.

According to Kimberly Tyson (2013), students *must know* Tier 2 academic vocabulary words. Knowing these words will help students be successful reading multiple texts across multiple subjects. Additionally, Jon Gustafson (2019) notes that Tier 2 words "fundamentally expand students' verbal functioning by building rich representations of words that can be used in a variety of contexts" (para. 18).

Domain-specific vocabulary refers to words that students encounter only when learning a specific topic within a specific subject. These are referred to as *Tier 3 words* by Beck, McKeown, and Kucan (2013). Words in the glossary of a text are usually domain-specific words. Examples are *photosynthesis*, *stamen*, and *monarchy*.

Tyson (2013) says that students *should know* Tier 3 words after reading texts that include them. However, as Gustafson (2019) points out, "These words have limited use outside the specific content area, and are not very helpful for enriching descriptions or explanations" (para. 15). These words tend to be the words in bold in textbooks. Authors emphasize these words so students can learn and understand specific concepts presented in text.

> Beck, McKeown, and Kucan (2013) also identified *Tier 1 words* as general oral vocabulary words. Students typically hear these words daily. They are not usually specific to content-area reading. *Push* and *pull* are examples of these words.

Vocabulary and Comprehension

Vocabulary knowledge contributes to reading comprehension. Logically, the more words a student knows, the better they will comprehend what they read. But it's not just about knowing a bunch of words. How well a student understands words also contributes to their comprehension. Vocabulary **breadth** refers to the number of words a person knows. Vocabulary **depth** refers to how well a person knows the words.

Research conducted by Katherine S. Binder et al. (2016) found that "both vocabulary breadth and depth were significantly correlated with reading comprehension and reading rate," and "a strong depth of vocabulary affects reading comprehension" (para. 1). Students who have deep understanding of words can comprehend text more readily than students without deep understanding.

Further, the depth of word knowledge goes beyond knowing definitions. It also includes "how it sounds (phonology), the written form (orthography), other forms of the word (morphology), its grammatical use (syntax), meanings and how it relates to other words (semantics), and how to convey meaning to others (pragmatics)" (Seifert 2015, para. 3). When students have depth of vocabulary knowledge, they can make word associations—connections between and among ideas. Students can also identify patterns between and among words when they have deep knowledge. The more students read, the greater exposure they have to vocabulary, increasing their likelihood of making meaning of text. (For information about wide reading, see page 58.)

Some vocabulary is more than a single word. **Word collocations** are two or more words that typically go together in context. For example, students may read about countries *waging war* or people inventing ways to *conserve energy*.

Vocabulary and Text Complexity

Vocabulary is one feature of language. It is also a key aspect of text complexity. As students move from one grade to the next, the vocabulary they enounter becomes increasingly complex. This naturally makes the text more complex as well. Sheena Hervey (2013) reminds us that texts with extensive academic vocabulary are more difficult to read. Hervey proposes that teachers must first realize what makes a text complex, then determine how best to help students construct meaning. To do this, teachers need to have a general understanding of how proficient their students are as readers, the complexity levels of the texts they will use, and what they will be doing with this new knowledge.

Implications for Teaching and Learning

Words are what we speak and listen to. Words are what we read, write, and comprehend. Word knowledge, or vocabulary, is essential for understanding text. Direct, explicit vocabulary instruction can help enhance and support reading comprehension. In addition to defining words, teachers should consider additional, meaningful, deep-learning activities when developing students' vocabulary.

Explicitly Teach Tier 2 Vocabulary

Students need explicit vocabulary instruction. Determining the words that students need is an integral component of vocabulary instruction. Sometimes, the key terms teachers should teach are not necessarily the words identified in textbooks and other reading materials, as these are often domain-specific, Tier 3 vocabulary words. Direct instruction of Tier 2 vocabulary will reap more benefits for students than teaching Tier 3 words. This is because academic words are more broadly used across the content areas and across contexts.

Tier 3 words are still needed for students to be successful with complex text and can often be told to students, reviewed quickly, or supported with vocabulary reference guides. Reference guides are miniature glossaries or dictionaries that provide students with key vocabulary they will need to be successful in reading a text. These can contain student-friendly definitions, pictures, or even charts. While reading a narrative piece, fourth-grade students encounter the term *butter churn*. While this word may confuse students, it isn't a high-utility word. Rather than engage in activities to support the understanding, a reference guide could easily define it and include a picture of a butter churn being used. As students encounter the word, they use the reference guide to quickly make sense of it and continue reading.

butter churn

As students, many of us dug into the dictionary when faced with unfamiliar words. Dictionary definitions are one way to teach vocabulary, but these are unlikely to help students understand the *meanings* of words and how to use them. According to Janis Harmon and Karen Wood (2018), some "content-specific words need more detailed and integrated instruction" for students to internalize and be able to work with key concepts and ideas (4). For example, the definition of *tradition* is "an inherited, established, or customary pattern of thought, action, or behavior (such as a religious practice or a social custom)" (Merriam-Webster, n.d.-c.). Although accurate, this definition will not likely have meaning for a class of second- or third-grade students. A better alternative is to provide or have students create student-friendly definitions for their words. In this example, students may explain *traditions* as "activities people do that their families have always done." Students can talk about or engage in activities that further articulate the meaning of the word to help them internalize it. They can list examples such as eating certain foods during certain holidays or having an outdoor movie night during the summer months.

Beyond identifying student-friendly definitions, teachers should provide students the opportunity to read the text(s) in which the words appear, discuss how the words relate to the definitions they created, and then determine if their definitions match the context. This allows students to clarify their meanings—changing, adding, or adjusting their definitions and examples.

Quickly engaging with definitions and reading words one time in context may still not be sufficient for students to have a deep understanding. Students should have time daily to actively engage in discussions and activities that support vocabulary acquisition. Suggestions for active engagement are included in figure 2.1. The examples show how a teacher may help students better understand the word *resource*.

Figure 2.1—Strategies to Engage Students with Vocabulary

Strategy	Description	Example
Picture Talk	Provide pictures showing how the word may be used in different contexts.	Ask, "Who might use this *resource*?" Show pictures of water, rocks, soil, and corn.
Demo This!	Conduct a short activity to demonstrate the word.	Take students outside to demonstrate how solar or wind energy can be used as a *renewable resource*.
Thumbs-up/ Thumbs-down	Read true or false statements related to the word. If the statement is true, have students show thumbs-up. If the statement is false, have students show thumbs-down. Call on students to justify their answers.	• All resources are used for energy. • All resources are natural. • People should conserve nonrenewable resources. • We have resources in our classroom.

This process of teaching students definitions and using thought-provoking, lively, interactive learning opportunities to engage with terms is often referred to as **robust vocabulary instruction**. This phrase was coined by Beck, McKeown, and Kucan in *Bringing Words to Life* (2013). They contend that Tier 2 words should be the focus of robust vocabulary instruction, as these are the words with the greatest utility over a range of content and contexts.

Include Word Study Opportunities

The English language is immense. As students rise in grade levels, they should be adding to their vocabularies. Knowing and using prefixes and suffixes can expand their vocabulary breadth and depth.

Reconsider the base word from the example above, *resource*. Knowing the meaning of this term may allow students to interpret and understand several other related terms in context: *resourceful*, *resourced*, *resources*, *resourcing*, *unresourceful*, *outsource*, and *crowdsource*.

One strategy for providing direct instruction in the use of root words, base words, prefixes, and suffixes (or *morphemes*, the smallest part of a word that carries meaning) is Word Study.

Susan Hanson and Jennifer Padua (n.d.) suggest a *process approach* "to teach students to know how to use their understanding of prefixes, suffixes, and root/base words to unlock the meaning of words." This strategy has three key components, as outlined in figure 2.2. This approach takes advantage of words in context, and it demonstrates for students the value of knowing and understanding word parts.

> " The unique vocabulary in informational text belongs to clusters where words have distinctive but conceptually interrelated meanings (e.g., acidic, abrasive, alkaline are all properties of substances). "
> —Elfrieda Hiebert (2013, 11)

base word—smallest group of letters that form a complete word (*rock, care, friend*)

root word—smallest group of letters that form an idea but need a prefix or suffix to form a word (*carn-, lum-, magni-*)

affix—word part added to the beginning (prefix) or ending (suffix) of a word (*dis-, pre-, un-, -able, -ful, -less*)

Figure 2.2—A Process Approach to Teaching Word Parts

Component	Example
Directly teach the meanings of base and root words with prefixes and suffixes. Show how prefixes and suffixes change the meanings of words.	The Latin root *sect-* means "cut." The prefix *inter-* means "between" or "among." When things *intersect*, they are divided where they meet.
Teach meaningful word parts explicitly as the need arises in the reading material.	Seventh-grade students read about a *dissection* to help scientists better understand how organs function. The teacher points out the root word to help students understand this word's meaning.
Model how to use context clues and word parts to make meaning.	Reading the word *sector* in context, students determine it means an area separate from other areas.

Similarly, Rasinski et al. suggest a simple strategy that opens the doors for learning multiple words: "By drawing a box around or otherwise highlighting the root that a group of words shares...you can give your students a 'root awakening'" (2020, 29). This awakening allows for students to discover words that have meaning connections due to their like word parts. Knowledge of word parts helps students build their store of vocabulary. This helps students recognize more words, leading to better reading comprehension.

Engage Students in Wide Reading

Wide reading is when students read several different texts on the same topic. This classroom practice deliberately builds students' vocabulary. Scott P. Ardoin et al. (2016) reflect that wide reading "exposes [students] to a significantly broader range of words" (34). By providing multiple texts that are appropriate for their reading levels, students are less likely to become bored or frustrated. As a bonus, this supports students when making connections between and among texts.

Key Terms for Teacher Understanding

Term and Definition	Example
academic vocabulary—words generally used in academic dialogue and text; Tier 2 words	Kyle's teacher asks students to *investigate* what happens when raisins are placed in clear soda. He remembers that he read about a historian *investigating* the disappearance of a World War II airplane pilot. He knows his teacher wants him to *look into* what happens with the raisins.
breadth of vocabulary knowledge—how many words a person has in their vocabulary; a general understanding of terms	Shandi read about tadpoles *emerging* from the water. She wasn't quite sure what this word meant, but she saw a picture of the creature moving from the water onto land. She concluded it must mean that the animal *comes out of* the water.
depth of vocabulary knowledge—the level of understanding of terms; being able to explain and relate a term to a specific and unique context	Mr. Vann asks students to give an example of something that has been *adapted*. He lists students' ideas on a chart, then guides them to think more deeply by asking, "Do you use an *adapter* on your devices? How might someone *adapt* to moving to a new country? What *adaptation* might you make to a go-cart?"
domain-specific vocabulary—words specific to a particular topic, subject, or concept; Tier 3 words	First-grade students used a diagram of a plant to identify the *leaf, flower, bud, root,* and *stem*.

Term and Definition	Example
robust vocabulary instruction—activities that engage students with words regularly and in varying contexts	Mrs. Lipton asks students to stand at their desks if they think something will *decrease* in each of these situations or sit if something will *increase*. • A boy withdraws money from his savings account. • A girl moves a container of ice cream from the freezer to the counter. • A Boy Scout places more wood on a fire. • A babysitter turns down the volume of the television. After each statement, she calls on one or more students to explain their thinking.
wide reading—reading several texts (perhaps different genres or with different text structures) about a topic	Students in Ms. Evian's second-grade class are learning about healthy eating habits. In addition to the section in their science textbooks, they read *Choose Good Food!* by Gina Bellisario and *Bread and Jam for Frances* by Russell and Lilian Hoban. They analyze diagrams identifying healthy meals. They look at food labels and find the amount of sugar, fat, and protein in some of their favorite snack foods.
word collocations—vocabulary that uses two or more words to communicate an idea	Mrs. Johnson's history class is learning the four features of a *sovereign state*. For a culminating activity, they create a fictional country and identify the features of their state.

Word Clusters

Grades: K–1

Description

Word Clusters reinforce vocabulary terms that have similar meanings. Word Clusters may be used to introduce new vocabulary or to practice and review related terms. Recording the activity provides students with a reference as their learning progresses.

Rationale

Word Clusters provide students with a hands-on way to say and understand vocabulary terms related to a specific topic. Since students collaborate to form the cluster, they have a safe environment to work with and manipulate the words.

Roles and Responsibilities

Teacher: Word Lister and Recorder

- Identifies words within a topic that have similar meanings.
- Defines unfamiliar terms.
- Records student responses.

Student: Organizer

- Clusters the words in a meaningful manner.

Process

Identify related terms within a topic of study or particular text. Write each of the words on its own note card. Review the words with the class, and hand each card to a student. Have students collaborate to place the words in a meaningful cluster. Gain consensus from the group. Encourage and support students to share other ideas for clustering the words. Once the cluster is complete, copy it onto a chart or display the cards on a bulletin board.

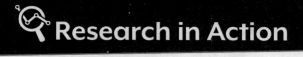

Differentiation

Draw pictures or place images of words students may not know on the cards. Have students talk with partners about connections they have to the words before clustering them.

In this example, kindergarten students are learning about Earth materials and how animals use them. After discussing and learning about different sizes of rocks, students cluster the words to show their progression from largest to smallest. They will add to this cluster when they learn about soil.

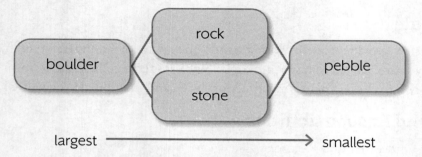

In this example, students have engaged with a piece of literature with the vocabulary word *furious*. Students use the Word Cluster to showcase the continuum of words that have similar meanings, identifying the shades of meaning.

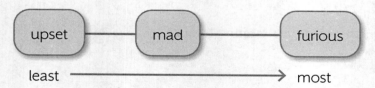

Connect Two

Grades: 2–3

Description

Connect Two allows students to make connections between words within a topic. Students collaborate with partners, providing a safe environment to consider relationships between words.

Rationale

Connect Two is a strategy that helps students develop a deeper understanding of vocabulary. Students should have a general understanding of either academic or domain-specific vocabulary before participating in this strategy.

Roles and Responsibilities

Teacher: Word Lister and Recorder

- Identifies academic and domain-specific words students will encounter in text.
- Reviews the meanings of the words as needed.
- Records student responses.

Student: Word Connector

- Identifies and describes the connection between two words.

Process

Identify academic and domain-specific terms within a topic of study. Write each word on a note card. (Each student will need a card, so some words may need to be written on more than one card.) Review the words with the class, and hand each card to a student. Have students collaborate to find a card another student has that is connected to or relates to their own cards. Develop a recording method, such as a chart or graphic organizer, for student responses.

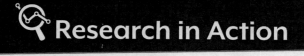
Research in Action

Differentiation

Post the sentence frames shown below. Draw pictures or place images of words on the cards. Discuss as a class or group where students encountered the words and how they are related to the topic. Challenge students to connect three or even four words and explain their relationship.

_____ and _____ are similar because _____.

_____ and _____ are different because _____.

_____ and _____ are related because _____.

_____ and _____ belong together because _____.

Word Rating

Description

Students in the intermediate grades can use a Word Rating to gauge their familiarity with essential vocabulary before they read a text. A Word Rating lists words students should know by the end of the unit. Students rate their familiarity with the words before reading, then again after reading and participating in vocabulary activities with the words. This is useful as a formative assessment during the learning process, and students may use it to identify words they did not learn after the learning process has concluded. Students can also use it to review before a summative assessment.

Rationale

A Word Rating provides a preview of the important vocabulary students will engage with during a specific text or unit of study. Students use prior knowledge and word parts (root words, prefixes, and suffixes) to showcase their knowledge of vocabulary before the unit takes place. Teachers use a Word Rating to set a purpose for reading, highlighting the words on the rating scale as must-learn vocabulary.

Roles and Responsibilities

Teacher: Word Identifier

- Creates the list with academic and domain-specific words students will encounter in texts.
- Shares the list with students.
- Collects information indicating student familiarity with words.
- Creates lessons for students to actively engage with the words.
- Provides time for students to evaluate their understanding of the words after learning and instruction.

Research in Action

Student: Self-reflector

- Indicates familiarity with the identified words.
- Revisits the vocabulary words throughout the learning process.
- Determines which words they need to review before a summative assessment.

Process

In this example, fifth-grade students are learning about a market economy. Both academic and domain-specific terms are in the first column. The ratings are beside each term. Students may use different-color pens or highlighters to indicate their understanding of the words before and after the unit. For example, they may use a blue highlighter to indicate their familiarity with each word before learning. At the conclusion of the unit, students may use a yellow highlighter to indicate how well they have learned each term.

Vocabulary Term	Know it well	Have seen/ heard it	Not yet	Definition
market economy				
supply				
demand				
goods				
services				
producer				
consumer				
scarcity				
capital resources				
human resources				

Note: Students may be familiar with the terms *producer* and *consumer* in the context of an energy pyramid. However, they may learn during reading that these particular academic terms have completely different meanings in the context of a market economy. For this reason, students should have opportunities to reflect orally and in writing to describe how their understanding of terms may have changed during the unit.

In primary grades, have students circle or color in a smiley, straight, or frowny face for each term. Doing this before and after learning will allow students to "see" their vocabulary grow.

Differentiation

Read aloud the words to students. Since this is a self-reflection, students should work independently when they initially complete their rating. However, as students continue to develop their vocabulary, provide opportunities for them to update their ratings and discuss the words with partners. Challenge students to write a definition, example, or clue next to each of the words as they are learning.

Alternate ratings could be:

> 0—I am not at all familiar with this word.
> 1—I have heard this but do not know what it means.
> 2—I have heard this but cannot explain it.
> 3—I have heard this and can kind of explain it.
> 4—I have heard this and understand what it means.
> 5—I have heard this, and I can teach others what it means.

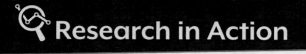

Kinesthetic Word Web

Secondary Grades

Description

This strategy turns a Word Web into an activity that incorporates movement. Teachers provide students with content information on index cards, and students create a Kinesthetic Word Web. Then, students may use the web as a springboard for a writing-in-response-to-reading activity.

Rationale

Movement is a helpful strategy when students are learning. Providing movement opportunities allows students to discover information for themselves and take an active role in their learning instead of having information simply presented to them verbally or visually.

Roles and Responsibilities

Teacher: Word Identifier

- Identifies academic and domain-specific words students will encounter in text.
- Reviews the meanings of the words as needed.

Student: Web Creator

- Collaborates to cluster words that belong together along with the main topic.

Process

Identify academic and domain-specific terms related to a topic or text. Write each main topic and each word on its own note card. Give each student a card (if you don't have enough, the students without cards can help organize their classmates). Have students walk around the room trying to determine which words are related to the words they have, and which word(s) is the main topic. Once a group believes they have found all of the related words, have the students form a circle with the main topic card in the center. The students in the circle each place one hand on the shoulder of the student with the main topic.

The example below shows how students can create two webs related to cell structure: one for plant cells and one for animal cells. Students will need to collaborate to ensure that only one of each common term is part of each cell type. This example allows for 20 students to actively participate.

- If you have more than 20 students, conduct the activity again so all students have a chance to actively participate.
- Making multiple sets of cards may create enough content for all students to participate.

Main Idea (center terms)	Vocabulary (circle terms)
plant cells	cytoplasm, chloroplast, vacuole, cell wall, Golgi body, ribosome, endoplasmic reticulum, cell membrane, nucleus, mitochondrion
animal cells	nucleus, Golgi apparatus, mitochondrion, cell membrane, ribosome, endoplasmic reticulum, cytoplasm, lysosome

Differentiation

- Provide a structure for the web by showing students how many words belong with each main idea.
- Have each group organize their web on a desk, and have the groups do a gallery walk to examine how other groups completed the web.
- Provide students time to generate words they can use to create their own webs.

Moving Forward: Top Must-Dos

Without an understanding of words, students will struggle to comprehend text with increasing complexity. Follow these steps to support student learning of the essential terms they need to be successful readers and writers.

Identify Academic and Domain-Specific Words Students Should Know

Remember that textbooks tend to highlight domain-specific words. Students need access to these words to comprehend complex texts and the ideas and concepts that texts explain and explore. However, these Tier 3 words should not necessarily be the focus of your direct vocabulary instruction. Instead, review student reading materials to locate key academic words. For example, young students learning about the seasons need to know the names of the seasons. *Autumn* may be a new word for them. Although it is specific to this unit of study, students will likely encounter it in the future, so it should be included as a key term. If the list is too long, decide which words to teach directly and which to clarify as they arise during instruction. Generally, three to five words are taught in one lesson. If the vocabulary list is longer than that, consider developing lessons where the words are taught in clusters of three to five each.

Explicitly Teach Vocabulary and Connect Words to Prior Knowledge

Teach vocabulary using definitions and examples, and connect words to prior knowledge. Once the list has been assembled, plan to directly teach the meanings of the words. Definitions should be student-friendly, perhaps created by students themselves if they have some familiarity with the words. Explain how the words are used in context by giving examples or discussing the context in which students will encounter the words. Doing this just once is not sufficient. Plan daily interactive activities where students can work with and use the words. The more involved students are with the activity, the more likely they will learn the definitions.

Incorporate a Word Study Component

Teaching students meaningful and useful base words, root words, and affixes will give them an advantage when learning other words with these components. For example, *geo-* is a common prefix students will see in both science and social studies vocabulary. Knowing that this prefix means "relating to Earth" will help students when they encounter it in an unknown word.

Further Considerations

One scaffold (or instructional support) teachers tend to provide when the vocabulary in a text is too complex is to simply read the text to students. Elfrieda Hiebert (2013) cautions that this practice is no longer a scaffold but is instead used as a regular routine. Hiebert states that "there is no evidence that shows that teachers' read-alouds of instructional/learning texts lead to increases in students' ability to read more fluently and proficiently in independent contexts." Students need the opportunity to grapple with complex texts to develop understanding. When students depend on their teachers to read for them, they cannot practice reading for automaticity, and therefore their willingness to read diminishes as texts become more complex.

Teachers should be mindful of how much reading they are doing compared to their students. This is a tricky balance and varies across grade levels. Teachers want students to learn the content, certainly. If the text available is too complex, a teacher's natural instinct is to read the text to students.

Hiebert offers these suggestions to help students practice reading and understanding complex text. First, remind students that they are responsible for reading and understanding the text. Second, strengthen their vocabulary knowledge. Third, increase the amount of time that students read daily. Another option when relying on text that is too complex is to embrace the practice of *wide reading* (see page 58).

My Teaching Checklist

Are you ready to develop students' vocabulary so they may be successful readers of complex texts? Use this checklist to help you get started!

Developing Vocabulary	
Look Fors	**Description**
Tier 2 words to target are identified.	• Look beyond the bold words in texts. • Identify words that have useful applications across content and across contexts.
The words are explicitly taught.	• Develop (or have students develop) student-friendly definitions. • Use daily interactive, meaningful, thought-provoking activities to help students develop deep understandings of terms.
Word study is incorporated.	• Teach how affixes affect the meanings of base and root words. • Point out word parts during reading. Help students make connections to other word parts they know.

Chapter Summary

Vocabulary is important. Without it, students cannot comprehend what they are reading. Domain-specific (Tier 3) words are essential for understanding specific content, but they should not be the sole focus of vocabulary instruction. Students will be more successful reading text when they deeply learn academic (Tier 2) words. These words are useful across content areas and in different contexts. Definitions are important, but they should be student-friendly. Students should have ample opportunities to engage with words, allowing them a greater likelihood of deeply understanding them.

Reflection Questions

1. How is vocabulary knowledge directly connected to comprehension?

2. How should you decide which words to teach students?

3. What are direct and indirect ways to teach students new words?

4. How will you know if students are deeply learning key terms?

Chapter 3

Literacy Knowledge: Print Concepts to Genre Study

Background Information and Research

One important facet of being a skilled reader is literacy knowledge, which provides a key foundation. It is often considered the basis for the emerging skills that allow students to read and write. Before students can begin to learn to read, they must first have some basic knowledge of how letters work, how sentences are formed, and ultimately, how print works. As literacy knowledge deepens, students develop an understanding of how different genres of literature are organized. This more complex literacy knowledge also plays into a student's ability to successfully read and comprehend. When students recognize a range of literary styles, they have a more developed framework and understanding of how text works. These ideas are explored more deeply in this chapter.

Literacy Knowledge is one of the integral topics on the Language Comprehension strand of Scarborough's Reading Rope (2001). This strand encompasses print concepts for early learners and expands to include nuances of various types of text through genre study. A term first coined by Marie Clay (1989), *concepts about print* (also known as *concepts of print* or *print awareness*), refers to ideas of what books and print are and how to navigate them in order to read. Once students have a fundamental understanding of print, the more complex understanding of how genre impacts text type and style becomes important in developing strong literacy knowledge.

Understanding Concepts of Print

Concepts of print are different from phonological awareness and phonics, although these three ideas are related. The Literacy Teaching Toolkit (Victoria State Government 2020) clearly explains their differences. When students have *print concepts*, they can, among other things, recognize symbols as letters, groups of letters as words, and groups of words as sentences. This skill is visual. When students have *phonological awareness*, they can hear the differences between words and sounds. This skill is completely auditory. When students use *phonics*, they can apply sounds to the symbols to form words. This skill is both visual and auditory.

Other ideas related to concepts of print include an understanding of the functions of a book or other text, print directionality, and knowing that print conveys a message. The main ideas related to concepts of print are explained in figure 3.1.

Figure 3.1—An Explanation of Concepts of Print

Concept of Print	Explanation	Example
Print conveys a message.	When we read, we make meaning of the words on the page.	A student correctly identifies the print to show where to start reading (instead of a picture).
Books are organized in a specific way.	Books have a front and back cover, and they should be held the right way up. They also include a title, an author, and perhaps an illustrator.	A student turns a book right-side-up when it is handed to them upside-down, and correctly identifies the front and back cover and the title and author.
Print is read in a specific way.	To read, we start in the upper left corner at the front of the book, sweep right across the page, then return to the left side on the next line of print. We turn pages from right to left, making our way to the back of the book.	A student correctly identifies where to begin reading on a page, tracks the text to the right across the page, then returns to the left on the next line. The student turns the page correctly to move on.

Concept of Print	Explanation	Example
Words are what we read.	Letters are symbols that we put together to make words. We put words together separated by spaces to make sentences. We use symbols to show when to pause and stop as we read.	A student correctly identifies a letter and word in print, how many letters make up a word, and how many words make up a sentence. The student correctly identifies and explains the purpose of a period, comma, exclamation point, and question mark.

Learning how to handle books correctly is one step in learning to read. This skill is important for all students. As the National Center on Early Childhood Development (2020) points out, "Children may develop print knowledge and learn how books work in a home language with a written form that is different from English" (6). Students can transfer their understanding of how books work in their first language to English. Likewise, students can transfer their understanding of print awareness: print, not pictures, tells the story no matter the language in which text is written.

Concepts of print for beginning readers are related to text features for children in first grade and beyond. Instead of focusing on letters, words, and sentences, students must learn how text features such as headings, captions, sidebars, pictures, and diagrams convey meaning. They can learn to use a table of contents, index, and glossary to locate information quickly. Correlations between concepts of print and text features are shown in figure 3.2.

A review of the research by Michelle J. Kelley and Nicki Clausen-Grace (2010) found that students do not automatically use text features. Students skip over them or do not use them to aid comprehension. But these features offer important information. Students must be taught what text features are and learn how they can support their comprehension when reading complex text. Knowing that the utility of text features and print concepts is low when students do not understand how to use them, educators must find engaging ways to teach the structure of print, language, and features, and allow for authentic practice in using them to support the understanding of text.

Figure 3.2—A Correlation between Concepts of Print and Text Features

Concept of Print	Text Feature
Print conveys a message.	Different text features convey messages.
Books are organized in a specific way.	Informational texts may have a table of contents, index, and glossary. Each has a specific location in the text.
Print works a specific way.	Informational texts use headings, subheadings, and bold and italicized words. These usually indicate key ideas that are important. Sidebars act to "call out" specific information within text.
Words are what we read.	We can "read" illustrations, images, and diagrams. They may have captions and labels for clarification.

The Digital Environment

Students are encountering digital environments and interacting with a range of digital media more and more frequently. In fact, many children engage with interactive media regularly, increasing the need for educators to consider related instructional implications. Students must develop and understand the nuances of digital print just as they need to understand print on paper. Many print concepts in a digital environment vary from print concepts for paper-based texts, meaning different skills are needed by students as they navigate digital texts. "E-books present interactive multimodal information such as written text, oral reading, music, illustrations, animations, and hotspots that are activated by touching or pressing the touch screen to generate sound and animation" (López-Escribano, Valverde-Montesino, Garcia-Ortega 2021, para. 3). Digital texts can open doors to literacy practices that are very different from those used when reading traditional texts. The language students use to discuss texts and how they access them expands as students learn to click screens, use arrow buttons to advance pages, watch text highlighting appear, locate icons to find eBooks, closely examine digital images, and use menu bars to save their favorite stories. It is important for teachers to recognize and teach concepts of digital print as they support their students in navigating digital texts.

Understanding Different Genres

A genre is a category or type of text. Every genre of text has its own purpose and structure. Texts within each genre are similar in form, style, and purpose. State and national language arts standards consistently reference and delineate the range of genres and the importance of skills and fluidity within these genres. The attention to genre is intentional. When teachers teach comprehension strategies generically, as though they apply in the same way to every type of text, students miss valuable information that supports their understanding. One common comprehension strategy is making predictions. When students engage with a story, they should ask, "What will *happen* next?" However, when reading informational text, this question is only valuable if the text uses a sequence structure. Rather, students benefit from considering questions such as "What will I *learn* next?" or "What other information will I gather in this section?" Further, some comprehension strategies are unique and offer specific supports to particular genres of text. Thus, ensuring that students know genre types and understand how different text types operate and function provides students with greater ability to understand and maneuver through a wide range of texts.

Literature refers to fictional stories, dramas, and poetry. Texts within each of these categories have typical organizational structures. For example, stories typically have characters, settings, and events that lead to an ending. Engaging students with story maps and activities to support event sequencing helps them understand the nuances of the genre. Under the umbrella of the literature genre, readers encounter drama. Dramas are stories written in dialogue. A narrator may tell "behind-the-scenes" information to the audience of readers, and information such as a change in scene may be presented in italics. Often considered the most concise form of literature, poetry can also describe a scene or tell a story.

> Ensuring that students know genre types and understand how different text types operate and function provides students with a greater ability to understand and maneuver through a wide range of texts.

Within each of these categories of literature, there are even more distinct genres. For example, literature encompasses adventure, historical fiction, mysteries, myths, fables, science fiction, realistic fiction, allegories, parodies, satire, and graphic novels. Dramas include one-act and multi-act plays. They may be in written or video form. Poetry includes several types of poems: narrative, lyrical, free-verse, sonnets, odes, ballads, and epics.

Informational texts are predominantly expository texts with print features such as captions, a table of contents, an index, diagrams, a glossary, and tables. Informational texts include biographies and autobiographies; books and articles about specific topics in history, economics, science, and the arts; technical texts including directions and forms; information in graphs, charts, and maps; and digital sources about specific topics. Students may also encounter expositions, arguments, personal and factual essays, speeches, opinions or op-eds, and memoirs, which can all be informational texts.

Building students' understanding of the nuances of different genres provides them knowledge to navigate different text types. This insight will support them as they read more than one text about a topic. In a blog post from *The Classroom Nook*, Rachael Parlett (n.d.) discusses how utilizing different genres has several advantages for students. First, students encounter a wide variety of vocabulary. In content areas, the key terms may be similar, but their explanations or uses may vary among texts. This provides students several opportunities to read and learn academic and domain-specific words. Second, students encounter different text structures. Each genre has its own organizational style, tone, and purpose. When students identify how different texts are structured, they may begin to make connections within and among texts. This concept is explored at length in Chapter 5. Also, students deepen their knowledge and understanding of the concepts under study when they read content presented in different genres.

Implications for Teaching and Learning

Print awareness is a foundational skill students must develop for success in navigating print. Teachers can model and instruct students for mastery in concepts of print in several ways. Students should learn that text features from a variety of genre types give valuable hints about a text's content and that they have important information that may not be expressed in the main text. It is imperative that students are exposed to and taught with a wide assortment of genres throughout their school experience. Using different genres of texts has far-reaching benefits for students, including that they may develop more knowledge and vocabulary and better comprehend content by reading various genres about related topics.

Promote Print Awareness

Since print awareness is an integral piece of literacy knowledge, ensuring students have adequate opportunities to develop their understanding of the functions and conventions of text is a foundational part of literacy work. There are myriad ways to enhance print awareness. It is imperative that instruction is intentional and designed for student mastery. Teachers begin promoting print awareness by labeling objects in the classroom. Further, teachers allow students to engage with texts, letter tiles or letter stamps, and sentence frames. Using predictable or pattern books provides students with practice mastering print concepts they have been taught through read-alouds and read-alongs.

"Big Books" are ideal for teaching print awareness. These oversized books allow for easy access by both teachers and students and offer ample modeling opportunities. Teachers may choose to read Big Books aloud, or, as students become more confident in their own reading, teachers may invite students to read the text to the group or class. Using the Big Book, the teacher models how to hold a book, turn the pages, and recognize the directionality of text. The teacher may also model effective fluency, pausing with punctuation or phrasing, and demonstrating prosody by changing inflection. Reading aloud also provides teachers opportunities to model print awareness concepts such as identifying letters, words, sentences, and punctuation. "Read-alouds help emergent and beginning readers gain understanding of book handling, print conventions, story structure, literacy syntax, expressive language, and text organizational structures" (International Literacy Association 2018, 3).

Additionally, students may read along with the teacher since the print in Big Books is large enough for them to see from a distance. This strategy still allows for modeling of reading techniques and concepts of print. However, students have the opportunity to try reading *with* the teacher in a non-threatening environment.

Both reading aloud and reading along show students that print is what we read. The teacher, when discussing pictures or other visuals on the pages, may explain how these features support the

> " Read-alouds help emergent and beginning readers gain understanding of book handling, print conventions, story structure, literacy syntax, expressive language, and text organizational structures. "
>
> —International Literacy Association (2018, 3)

text. Students may join conversations about the text and feel a sense of ownership in their reading.

Predictable or pattern texts use repetitive language so early readers may practice the structures of text within books. They are able to practice directionality, the skills of identifying letters and words, and locating punctuation. Students recognize words on the page and decipher sentences.

Ideally, any opportunity teachers have to immerse children in print supports print awareness. Beyond just labeling the room, ideas include manipulating letter tiles; reading signs, posters, menus, or other "environmental print"; and having students write often for various purposes, such as personal letters, postcards, and journals.

Using sticky notes on a Big Book to identify letters

Teach Different Genres

As students read more and more, they may begin to instinctively identify differences in texts. For example, students may read a mystery and understand that it has a special kind of situation and ending that is different from other stories. But they should know the characteristics of mysteries in order to identify one the next time they read one. This requires teachers to explicitly teach students structures and features of different genres.

As early as first grade, students should learn to identify *fiction* and *nonfiction* texts. Within the fiction category, students learn the difference between *realistic fiction* and *fantasy*. As students rise through the grades, teachers can add to students' understanding of more genres. National and state reading standards list specific genres students should learn about and read.

Teachers can plan lessons to specifically teach each genre. One way teachers can help students keep track of the genres they learn is to begin and add to an anchor chart listing the genres, the characteristics, and text titles as students learn about them. Students can collaborate in small groups to sort books based on the genres they have learned. Teachers in upper grades may consider creating a genre scavenger hunt by listing the genres students need to explore and leaving room for students to list the titles they discover.

Teach Text Features

Be sure students read the obvious! Text features such as headers and sidebars are quite valuable in helping students comprehend complex text, and they are usually prominently displayed on the page. Kelley and Clausen-Grace (2010) suggest conducting a "Text Feature Walk" to introduce new informational text. This process is similar to conducting a picture walk, but instead students preview text features they will encounter during reading. Students can see how information is "chunked," a supportive reading strategy. Students can make predictions about the content and discuss how the features support the main ideas and details. After reading, they may reflect on how attending to the text features supported their understanding of the content.

Key Terms for Teacher Understanding

Term and Definition	Example
genre—category or type of text differentiated by format, style, and topic	Mrs. Ling introduces the term *biography*. After a brief discussion about what students know about this term, she provides small groups of students several examples of biographies. Students collaborate to identify characteristics of these texts, which the class uses to develop a student-friendly definition of the term.

Term and Definition	Example
informational text—one category of nonfiction that informs readers about a particular topic	At the start of the school year, Mr. Phillips sends his students on a scavenger hunt for different informational texts they will use during the school year. He has them identify the titles of specific chapters, definitions of specific words in glossaries, and the topics supported by charts and other diagrams.
literature—text in the form of fictional prose, drama, or poetry	Once a month, Ms. Fields has a "Book Club Lunch" with students who are all reading the same piece of literature. The group discusses different scenes and what aspects resonated with students.
print awareness—also referred to as *concepts of print*; beginning reading skills related to how books are organized and how text within books shares a message	Mr. Popp introduces a Big Book about insects. He calls on students to identify the front and back covers and the title and author (which he reads aloud). After reading the text through once, he revisits pages to have students point to the text and show how to read the words across the page.
read-along—instructional strategy where the teacher guides students to read aloud with them (choral read)	During small-group instruction, the students in Mr. Andrews' small group will reread a text they read yesterday. Students point to the words as they read them aloud. Mr. Andrews makes note of words students stumble over to practice as part of a phonics lesson or to add to their sight vocabulary.
read-aloud—instructional strategy where the teacher reads text aloud to students to model appropriate reading skills	Mrs. Bond chooses a short picture book about friendship to read aloud to students. She jots notes to herself and places them on the pages where she wants to stop and model how she can use her own thinking and the text to make inferences.

Big Book Read-Aloud

Grades: K–1

Description

A Big Book Read-Aloud is a teacher-led, interactive strategy where the teacher models concepts of print while asking questions of students or having them repeat what the teacher did. This strategy may also be used with picture books or during small-group instruction.

Rationale

A Big Book Read-Aloud shows students how print works and how readers "read." Students are active participants by responding to questions about specific concepts or functions of print or mirroring print concepts modeled by the teacher.

Roles and Responsibilities

Teacher: Big Book Reader

- Finds a fiction or nonfiction Big Book to use.
- Models concepts of print with a read-aloud.
- Uses some of the following tools to support the read-aloud:
  - ❖ pointer
  - ❖ highlighter tape
  - ❖ Wikki Stix®
  - ❖ sticky notes
  - ❖ sentence strips

Student: Listener

- Follows along with the teacher.
- Answers questions about print concepts.
- Mirrors print concepts modeled by the teacher.

Research in Action

Process

Display the Big Book in a prominent area where all students can see it. Use a pointer or other tool to point to certain features and model sweeping left to right and return sweep to the next line.

Prompts for a Big Book Read-Aloud include these:

- Display the book upside down or backward and ask, "What's wrong?"
- Ask why someone's name is on the book.
- Have students locate the title, author, and illustrator of the book.
- Ask, "Where is the print?" or "Where should I begin reading?"
- Prompt students to locate a letter, a sentence, or punctuation within the text.
- Search for capital letters, punctuation, or pictures, and use highlighter tape to mark them.

Differentiation

Call on students to repeat what you modeled, such as return sweep or page turning. Use highlighter tape or other tools to identify letters, words, and sentences, then have students count the letters in a word and words in a sentence. Have students use hand signals to indicate what to do when they see punctuation. For example, they can put their hands up to show "stop" for a period or shrug their shoulders when they come to a question mark.

Title Sort

Grades: K–1

Description

A Title Sort is an interactive strategy where students analyze books and determine if they are fiction or nonfiction. A two-column chart can be used to record the titles for a review of the differences between these two types of texts.

Rationale

Title Sorts are a hands-on way for students to compare texts and identify them as fiction or nonfiction. Students collaborate to sort books, providing a safe environment in which to discuss, compare, and categorize.

Roles and Responsibilities

Teacher: Book Finder and Recorder

- Identifies suitable books for students to sort.
- Records titles in a two-column chart.

Student: Sorter

- Analyzes and compares books.
- Sorts books based on their characteristics.

Process

Provide each pair or small group of students four or five books to sort—some fiction and some nonfiction. Instruct students to look at the books, discuss them, and then decide if they are fiction or nonfiction and sort them into two piles. Have each group share how they know which books are fiction and which books are nonfiction. Record some titles of each type of book on a two-column chart, if desired. Discuss whether or not students can identify books as fiction or nonfiction based on their titles alone.

Research in Action

Differentiation

Provide each pair or small group with one of each type of book to sort. Point out features of each book, such as dialogue, headings, and the types of pictures they have. Remind students of the features of each type of book. Use an anchor chart to support students as they discern between the types of text.

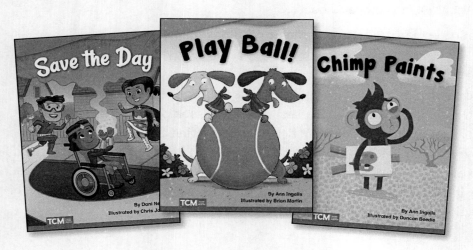

Genre Wheel

Grades: 2–3

Description

A Genre Wheel is a circle divided into sections, with each section listing a different genre, including fiction and nonfiction. Students use the wheel to track the genre types they have engaged with during independent reading.

Rationale

A Genre Wheel provides students with a tangible reminder to choose different types of text during independent reading. This strategy supports students in discovering, identifying, and reading different genres.

Roles and Responsibilities

Teacher: Wheel Maker

- Provides a Genre Wheel for each student to keep with their reading log.

Student: Decider

- Uses the wheel to identify which genre to read next during independent reading.

Process

Create a Genre Wheel using paper, and provide a copy to each student. Each student can independently select their reading choice from one of the genres and mark the wheel to indicate which genre they have selected. Students select their next reading choices from one of the remaining genres.

Differentiation

Students may color in the space on the wheel to indicate that they have read that genre. For a game of chance, add spinners to the Genre Wheels so students can spin their wheels to allow chance to determine their next genre type. Set clear expectations for the number of genres students should read in a given amount of time. Another option is a Genre Tic-Tac-Toe board. Students must read the

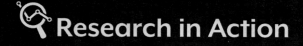
three different genres listed in one row, column, or diagonal on the board. A third option is to find a tool online that students may access, such as one from Wheel Decide (**wheeldecide.com**) or Wordwall (**wordwall.net**).

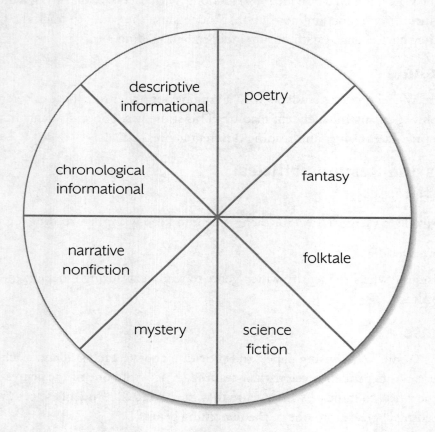

Genre Study

Grades: 4–5

Description

Throughout the year, students engage with a series of lessons to help them identify characteristics of different genres. During a Genre Study, students compare and contrast texts within the same genre. These texts may be collated from a unit of study to reinforce genre instruction.

Rationale

A Genre Study explicitly teaches students to compare and contrast ideas within the same genre to build understanding. In working with literature, students often analyze emotions, perspectives, and themes. Similarly, students use different informational texts to ascertain varying accounts, perspectives, and additional information.

Roles and Responsibilities

Teacher: Lesson Developer

- Plans lessons and activities to have students compare and contrast texts within the same genre, with similar themes or topics.
- Makes a class chart of information gathered in the comparison of the various texts or has students record it in their reader notebooks.

Student: Reader

- Reads books or texts in the genre being compared and contrasted.
- Records evidence from the book or text to demonstrate the characteristics of that particular genre.

Process

Provide multiple texts within the same genre. Provide organizers such as Venn diagrams for students to use to showcase similarities and differences between the texts.

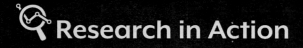 **Research in Action**

Differentiation

Support multiple modalities by having students listen to audio recordings, such as songs, speeches, or interviews of the people they are reading about. Encourage students to look for other texts (besides books) related to their topics, such as magazine articles or blog posts. Use this opportunity to identify first- and third-person points of view.

Multiple Perspectives

Secondary Grades

Description

With this strategy, students have access to multiple resources about a specific topic. They read and review each resource, then reflect on what they learned by responding to the question, "How do these sources represent different perspectives about [this topic]?"

Rationale

Assigning students reading selections and other informational texts that encompass multiple perspectives helps them think critically about a topic. Students are valued for determining various perspectives about a specific topic.

Roles and Responsibilities

Teacher: Questioner

- Poses a key question that can be answered through multiple perspectives.

Student: Researcher

- Reads multiple texts from diverse perspectives about the topic.
- Identifies diverse perspectives.

Process

Pose an open-ended, thought-provoking question about a topic of study, such as, "Which country was the most influential during the Industrial Revolution?" Provide informational texts and other resources students may use to conduct their research. Encourage the use of both text and audio-visual resources. Have students report on the different perspectives through group work, discussion, and writing.

Differentiation

Provide texts at varying reading levels and with supportive text features for students who need support reading complex texts. Provide links to online resources that students may find helpful when conducting their research. Have students reflect in writing to explain how the diverse resources represent the various perspectives about the topic.

Moving Forward: Top Must-Dos

Teachers can utilize a multitude of classroom strategies and activities to support all students' literacy knowledge.

Promote Literacy Knowledge with a Print-Rich Environment

Early readers benefit from being surrounded by text. A print-rich classroom allows students to interact with (and produce) a multitude of texts. An inviting reading area encourages students to explore texts of their choice comfortably. Environmental print allows students to read familiar text. These are everyday printed materials that students encounter around them, such as signs, labels, and logos. And the teacher can immerse students in texts by frequently modeling the process of reading using different age-appropriate genres.

Students in upper grades will benefit from a print-rich environment when they have easy access to different genres of text. Displaying a range of texts encourages students to explore many options within the classroom. Posting relevant vocabulary (with definitions and illustrations or examples) on classroom walls gives students ready access to key terms they are learning. Learning walls allow for students to engage with their recently acquired knowledge and vocabulary as they continue learning. Displaying written student work shows that their work is valued, and it supports what they are learning. Written directions for specific tasks provide support for students who might forget directions provided only in an auditory manner.

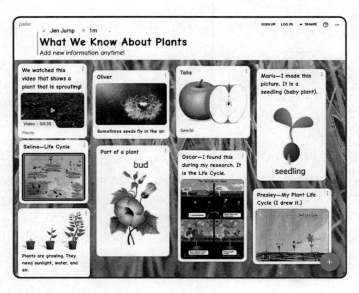

Use Read-Alouds and Shared Reading Daily to Teach Print Concepts

Students who are beginning readers need explicit instruction in concepts of print. Teacher read-alouds let students see and participate in ideas related to book handling and print concepts such as identifying the title and author. Teachers can explain how letters, words, and sentences are displayed and work together in print. Using a pointer allows the teacher to model correct reading across the page with return sweep.

Shared reading engages students as active participants. They can point to the first and last words on a page, turn the pages, and highlight different text features and symbols. These steps in the gradual release of responsibility provide the practice opportunities for students to be able to engage with print independently. Students can also read short poems, rhymes, or songs. These short texts allow for students to practice the concepts and functions of print with more independence.

Teach Students about Different Genres

In addition to addressing essential national and state reading standards, teaching students about different genres broadens their understanding of texts, and it can help them identify their reading preferences. Since each genre is categorized based on its characteristics, a natural progression is to infuse instruction on various text features.

> Access to new genres and formats introduces students to new literature types and forms. Providing access to these literature types also allows students to uncover their unique features and offerings while appreciating the elements of each.
>
> —Angie Zapata, Monica Kleekamp, and Christina King (2018, 4)

Explicitly teaching different genres also gives teachers flexibility in planning content-area lessons because they may incorporate different genres into a topic of study. In doing so, teachers may help students make connections among different texts and improve their vocabulary skills, which in turn builds knowledge in general. Additionally, using different genres allows students access to various text options which may be better aligned with their reading levels and skills.

Beyond explicit lessons teaching the various genres of text, students can learn about and experience genres through read-alouds. Students of all grade levels and within each content area can engage with a range of genres. "Access to new genres and formats introduces students to new literature types and forms. Providing access to these literature types also allows students to uncover their unique features and offerings while appreciating the elements of each" (Zapata, Kleekamp, and King 2018, 4).

Further Considerations

Remember that genres fall into two main categories: fiction and nonfiction. Beginning in first grade, students should delve a little more deeply into these two categories. National and state reading standards identify at each grade level specific genres students should read. Teachers should plan multiple opportunities for students to read each genre. And students should be able to identify genres based on the texts' characteristics. Nonfiction Big Books are suitable options for teaching features of informational texts in primary grades.

Teachers in primary grades should carefully consider the texts they will use to teach students concepts of print. Pattern and predictable books can be useful for this purpose. But decodable books are better options when teaching students phonics, and they may also be used to teach concepts of print. Teachers can model concepts of print using Big Books and trade books used as read-alouds as well.

My Teaching Checklist

Are you ready to develop students' literacy knowledge so they may be successful readers of complex texts? Use this checklist to help you get started!

Developing Literacy Knowledge	
Look Fors	**Description**
Students are immersed in print and texts.	• Label items and pictures that support learning. • Display a number of different genres and text types. • Provide a multitude of reading and writing experiences.
Read-alouds are used to teach concepts of print.	• Select books to teach concepts of print. (Upper-grade teachers can teach text features.) • Ask relevant questions to develop concepts of print (or identify how text features support information).
Students have opportunities to read and learn about different genres.	• Teach students specific characteristics of different genres. • Have students read, analyze, and evaluate different genres. • Upper-grade students may begin to make connections among texts.

Chapter Summary

Students must have basic literacy knowledge of concepts of print to begin learning to read. Teachers in early grades can model how to handle books and how print works during read-alouds. Literacy knowledge is also related to students' understanding of different genres. As students learn about different genres, teachers provide instruction about text features, and students may make connections among different texts. The more knowledge students have about basic literacy skills, the more confident they may be when required to read various texts to build knowledge, learn new vocabulary, and understand new ideas and concepts.

Reflection Questions

1. What did you already know about literacy knowledge that was confirmed in this chapter?

2. Which idea did you think more carefully about when reading this chapter? Why?

3. Explain how you will implement one strategy related to literacy knowledge in your classroom.

Chapter 4

Language Structures: Syntax and Semantics

Background Information and Research

Early on, children learn that words communicate meaning. Words are organized in a specific order to create a complete thought. With command of the structure of language, we are able to communicate both verbally and in writing. Merriam-Webster (n.d.-a.) defines *language* as "the words, their pronunciation, and the methods of combining them used and understood by a community." English words are organized in a particular manner that can be confusing and perplexing. For example, consider this sentence: "The brown fox jumped over the lazy dog." The order of words implies the fox is brown, the dog is lazy, and the fox jumped over the dog. Without syntactic understanding, this may be interpreted differently. Perhaps both the fox and the dog are brown and lazy. Couple this with the English use of phrases, figures of speech, idioms, and puns; it's no wonder students often grapple with comprehending complex uses of the English language. For example, "The brown fox, trying not to blow his chance at escape, jumped over the lazy dog." How does one "blow a chance?" This seemingly simple modification to the sentence may make understanding the information difficult for some students. This raises the question, can reading difficulties be related to syntactic misunderstandings (i.e., the structures within language)? This chapter explores in depth how the structures of language contribute to students' reading comprehension.

> The English language follows a strict set of rules that are expansive and complex.

Language Structures is another key component on the Language Comprehension upper strand of Scarborough's Reading Rope (Scarborough 2001). Words in text express ideas using language. Understanding how we structure language, therefore, is a key part of comprehending what we read. This strand may be divided into two categories: **syntax** (sentence structure) and **semantics** (nuanced meanings). Together, they make up *language*, which students produce and comprehend both verbally and contextually.

The Structure and Function of Language

The English language follows a strict set of rules that are expansive and complex. According to Robin Aronow and K. Bannar (n.d.), "Verbs are the central component of any utterance" (para. 3). Sentences are arranged in a specific grammatical structure. For example, you might say, "Emma read a book." But you would not say, "A book read Emma." The syntactic structure of the words in the sentence is restricted by the verb *read*. However, you might say, "A book was read by Emma." This changes the sentence to passive voice, which may confuse readers as to who is doing what, even though the meaning is the same as in the first sentence. These nuances and complexities can make understanding text very difficult for students.

For students to have the best skill set to attack a range of texts, they must understand that the arrangement of words in a sentence determines its meaning. As Jennifer Wagner (n.d.) states, "Thematic roles are the semantic relationships between the verbs and noun phrases of sentences." For example, figure 4.1 describes the thematic roles, also referred to as *arguments*, of the noun phrases in the sentence, "The boy places the plate of cookies on the counter." Each noun or noun phrase has a semantic relationship to the verb, *places*.

Figure 4.1—Thematic Roles of Noun Phrases

Noun or Noun Phrase	Theme	Description
the boy	agent	the entity performing the action
the plate of cookies	theme	the entity that directly receives the action of the verb
on the counter	goal	the place where the action is directed

Students read words that an author has strategically structured in order to convey meaning. Both the order of the words and the relationships among the words contribute to students' comprehension of the text. As expressed by Louisa Cook Moats (2020), "The nature of meaning will be considered at the word level (**lexical semantics**), at the phrase and sentence level (**sentential semantics**), and by a brief look at the supports for meaning-making residing with a social context (**pragmatics**)" (216). We will explore these ideas further as we closely investigate both syntax and semantics and their roles in comprehending English.

Syntax

Syntax refers to the arrangement of words and phrases to form meaningful sentences. In English, most simple statements follow a subject-predicate or subject-predicate-object construction: Birds chirp; Scissors cut paper; Tape sticks. We may add adjectives, adverbs, or phrases to embellish our ideas: Birds chirp loudly; Sharp scissors cut paper easily; Tape sticks to most surfaces. All these remain simple sentences. They have one subject and one predicate. Language gets fancy when we add clauses: Birds chirp loudly when the sun comes up; Sharp scissors cut paper easily most of the time; Tape, if used properly, sticks to most surfaces. Adding a clause changes a simple sentence to a complex sentence. Language becomes more complex when two complete sentences are combined to form one compound sentence: Birds chirp loudly when the sun comes up, thus sounding the alarm that a new day has begun. Notice that each of these embellishments deepens the complexity of the text, which may make it more challenging to comprehend.

Figure 4.2—Relationship among Words and Their Construction

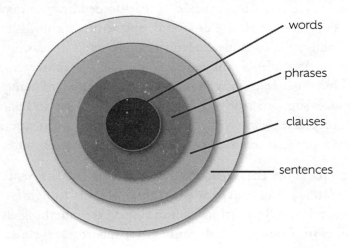

103

The relationship among these features of sentence construction is shown in figure 4.2. This image is a simplistic representation of how we construct language; we can further subdivide each category. For example, consider the types of sentences we form using words, phrases, and clauses (figure 4.3).

Figure 4.3—Subcategories of Sentence Structures

Structure	Description	Example
simple	one independent clause	Cats chase mice.
compound	two independent clauses separated by a semicolon or by a comma with a conjunction	Cats chase mice, and the mice scatter.
complex	one independent clause and one or more dependent clauses	When the mice scatter, the cats do not give up.
compound-complex	two independent clauses and one or more dependent clauses	Although the cats keep trying, the mice are very fast, and the cats are unsuccessful.

According to Pamela Snow (2021), "syntactic competency, receptively and expressively, enables children and adolescents to both construct and process increasingly complex ideas via the increased range afforded by grammatical structures such as negatives, reflexive pronouns, and sentence embedding" (230). Teachers have an obligation to guide students to understand increasingly complex texts. Teachers can help students pull sentences apart and learn to recognize the components and how they interact with one another. The skill of being able to manipulate sentences supports students in pulling out the topic and point of the sentence (subject-predicate; who or what did what?). In fact, when students filter through the phrases and clauses, the main idea of the sentence becomes clearer.

Consider the example about the brown fox and lazy dog. The first sentence, a simple sentence (and also an **independent clause**), is fairly straightforward. Something (a brown fox) did something (jumped over) to something else (a lazy dog). The second example includes a **dependent** (or subordinate) **clause**. The words *trying not to blow his chance at escape* cannot stand alone as a complete thought. They depend on the independent clause to make sense.

Louisa Moats (2020) asserts that knowledge of syntax is critical for reading and writing, explaining that poor readers "tend to struggle with sentence form and meaning, and benefit from explicit instruction in how sentences work" (182). She proposes that teachers provide guidance and practice in taking sentences apart, unpacking the meanings of sentences, and linking each part of a sentence to its overall meaning. This includes explicit instruction in grammar (noun-verb agreement related to tense, number, and person, and pronouns and their referents), parts of speech, types of phrases (e.g., noun, verb, adjective, and prepositional), types of clauses (e.g., independent and dependent), and types of sentences (e.g., simple, complex, and compound). For strategies and suggestions related to teaching syntax, see "Implications for Teaching and Learning" beginning on page 109.

> A **subordinate clause** is not a complete sentence, but it does have a subject and a verb. A subordinate clause may take on the role of an adjective, adverb, or noun. A subordinating conjunction, such as *although* or *until*, or a relative pronoun, such as *which* or *whose*, sets off the clause.

Semantics

Semantics refers to the meanings of words, phrases, and sentences. Since many words in English have similar meanings, and there is more than one way to express a single idea, students need to have a solid understanding of how words and the words that make up phrases and clauses work together to form meaning.

Students can learn the meanings of words, but they must apply them to some context to make meaning. For example, consider these sentences:

- The base is off center.
- He almost hit a crane.
- The case was wild.

Each of these simple sentences is grammatically correct. But how did you interpret their meaning? Was the *base* home plate or the bottom of a structure? Was the *crane* a bird or a piece of large equipment? Was the *case* an event or a small box? Without context, readers may interpret each sentence differently.

Language to Build Vocabulary

Jessie Ricketts et al. (2016) found that contextual support benefits emergent readers both when reading words that are phonetically based (regular) and when reading words that do not follow phonetic rules (exception words). They "observed an interaction between context and word type such that sentence context particularly facilitated reading of exception words" (340). Recognizing and reading words in isolation builds reading fluency. When students encounter words in context, they may determine meanings of familiar words used in unfamiliar ways. For example, when reading about energy-producing *plants* (for coal, natural gas, and the like), students may become confused if they have never encountered the word *plant* when it means "factory." Even if the text is easily decodable, students may struggle to comprehend the information if they do not stop and consider the new meaning of *plant* in this context.

Aside from learning multiple-meaning words, students can add to their store of vocabulary by learning about and identifying synonyms and antonyms. This allows students to have more options when describing meanings of lesser-known words. For example, students reading about a predator *devouring* prey may not fully understand what is happening. An explanation may be provided using similar ideas, such as a hungry puppy *wolfing down* his food, or a child *gobbling up* a bowl of ice cream. If similar meanings are unclear, we can turn to opposite meanings to offer explanations. For example, if someone has a *bitter* look in their eyes, they are not pleased.

> Understanding relationships among words allows for more specificity when describing people or situations, and it can lead to better comprehension of characters' actions and how they contribute to a story.

Regular experiences with synonyms also provide the construct for teaching nuances in word meanings. Understanding relationships among words allows for more specificity when describing people or situations, and it can lead to better comprehension of characters' actions and how they contribute to a story. For example, is a character feeling *worried* or *frantic*? Is the situation *bleak* or *miserable*? The more understanding students have of nuanced words, the more accurately they may interact with and respond to texts.

Teachers may explicitly teach relationships among words by identifying words to target in context. During reading, the teacher may stop and discuss the target words, relying on the events and characters' actions to support the words' meanings. Then, students may share additional experiences related to the words. For example, if students encounter the target word *melancholy* in a story, the teacher might ask, "What is happening at this point in the story? How can we use this event to figure out how [this character] is feeling? When is another time you or someone you know might have been *melancholy*?"

When Language Doesn't Follow the Rules

Figurative language is a broad category of uses of words that diverge from the literal meanings. It includes figures of speech, sound devices, and imagery. Generally, people imply the use of personification, idioms, similes, metaphors, and hyperbole when they describe figurative language. However, everyday English uses some figurative meanings of words that don't necessarily fit these categories. Consider the example earlier in the chapter, "blow a chance." No one can literally *blow* a chance. This phrase just means that someone lost an opportunity. Likewise, what does it mean to "get crackin'"? No one is *cracking* anything. It just means to get started doing something. While students do not need to be fully equipped with the complete etymology of figurative language, they should have knowledge of these types of phrases so they may grasp their meanings and comprehend the content of the text in which they appear. Definitions and examples of common figurative language literary devices are shown in figure 4.4.

> Mila Vulchanova et al. (2019) "discuss three factors that influence idiom comprehension: idiom decomposability, familiarity, and supportive context," (369) where *decomposability* refers to the relationship between the literal lexical meanings of individual words in an idiom and their overall phrase meaning.

Figure 4.4—Definitions and Examples of Common Figurative Language

Type	Definition	Examples
hyperbole	exaggeration	If I've told you once, *I've told you a billion times*, don't exaggerate!
idiom	non-literal phrase	The *cat's out of the bag.* Are you *pulling my leg*?
metaphor	implied comparison between two things	My sister is a *night owl.* You make *a better door than a window.*
personification	human characteristics expressed by non-human subjects	The floors *groaned.* The wind *howled.*
simile	comparison using *like* or *as*	He's *as strong as an ox.* Watching this movie is *like watching paint dry.*

Authors use figurative language to evoke particular emotions or creatively drive home certain points. When students encounter language that does not mean what it says, they may miss important information and lack full comprehension. Teachers cannot teach students every idiom or every figure of speech. They can, however, directly teach these literary devices and teach students to identify and analyze them in context in order to maximize their comprehension when reading text independently.

Implications for Teaching and Learning

Since both syntax and semantics play a role in language, to learn to comprehend more complex texts effectively, students should have direct instruction in both the structure of language and how it constructs meaning. Grammar and composition instruction does not need to be rote, boring, or mundane. Teaching these is exceptionally powerful when teachers can teach within the reading students are doing within any content area. Teachers can also use game-like strategies to turn practice into play. Additionally, shared language is a strategy that encourages students to be active participants. Students orally contribute to the class or group task, and the teacher transcribes their contribution, providing support as needed to compose grammatically correct sentences. Consider the following ideas when planning meaningful language lessons and activities.

Explicitly Teach Grammar and Syntax

More complex sentences place higher comprehension demands on students. When sentences "follow the rules," the text is cohesive, and students may better understand the information or message. Providing students with explicit instruction in how to recognize and interpret sentence parts allows students to understand key aspects of the topic, such as when, how, or why something occurs. Moats (2020) identifies these key grammar components to teach explicitly to students:

- parts of speech
- phrases
- subject/predicate
- independent/dependent clauses
- conjunctions and signal words that introduce and combine phrases and clauses

She also suggests providing practice with combining sentences. Teachers can design focused mini-lessons on each type of sentence, and students can combine sentence strips with words, phrases, and clauses to model each type.

Teachers can use games, such as bingo or Jeopardy®, to review and practice grammar-related topics. Additionally, there are many online practice games students may use to develop and solidify their grammar skills. Funbrain (grades pre-K to 8) and Freerice (grades 5 to 12) are two such examples.

Include Semantic Meaning Opportunities

One strategy for teaching word meanings is to use word webs or word maps. This idea was explored in Chapter 1. Word webs can also be used to teach the meanings of phrases. Essentially, the unknown word or phrase is placed in a circle in the center of the page, and related words and pictures are added around the word to help students learn the meaning. Once completed, the related words may be used in future lessons where students categorize or sort words based on their shared attributes. The related words may also be used to teach shades of meaning. Students can order the words from general to specific, or pair words with similar or opposite meanings. Teachers can partner students and ask questions for them to discuss related to the words and their meanings. For example, *When is a time you felt* exhausted? *Would you ever want to encounter a* sinister *animal? Who is the most* influential *person you know?*

> Grammar and composition instruction does not need to be rote, boring, or mundane. Teaching these is exceptionally powerful when teachers can teach within the reading students are doing within any content area.

To help students comprehend longer (and more complex) sentences, teachers can show students how to "chunk" phrases to better make meaning of text. Consider this example from the chapter "Greater Roadrunner" in *Danger in the Desert* by Timothy J. Bradley (2013, 14).

> The greater roadrunner can fly, but it prefers to run on the ground with its strong legs. This two-foot-long bird can be found in North American deserts racing across the rocky terrain in search of a meal. The roadrunner feeds on insects, reptiles, and small birds. Greater roadrunners can run about 20 miles per hour when chasing prey. They grab their prey in their strong beaks and beat it against the ground until it's dead.

Now, reread the text by chunking phrases:

> The greater roadrunner can fly,
>
> but it prefers to run
>
> on the ground
>
> with its strong legs.
>
> This two-foot-long bird
>
> can be found
>
> in North American deserts
>
> racing across the rocky terrain
>
> in search of a meal.
>
> The roadrunner feeds
>
> on insects, reptiles, and small birds.
>
> Greater roadrunners can run
>
> about 20 miles per hour
>
> when chasing prey.
>
> They grab their prey
>
> in their strong beaks
>
> and beat it against the ground
>
> until it's dead.

Notice how reading and pausing between phrases allows the reader to consider the words more carefully and improve comprehension. This strategy shows students how chunking text can make complex structures easier to navigate.

Directly Teach Figurative Language

Students who comprehend figurative language and other figures of speech may have an easier time understanding text more deeply. Students who are able to analyze relationships, especially those that are non-literal, conceptualize ideas more clearly. Each type of figurative language may first be taught out of context, then identified in context. Poetry and song lyrics tend to have appropriate examples of different literary devices.

Once students know about different types of literary devices, teachers may again use student-centered activities and games for learning and practice. For example, students can match literal meanings to their figurative meanings; play "I Spy" by identifying various literary devices when reading stories and novels; or describe characters, settings, or events using assigned devices. Regular practice will help students identify and comprehend these words and phrases in context.

Key Terms for Teacher Understanding

Term and Definition	Example
figurative language—words and phrases used non-literally for effect	Fourth-grade students describe different situations when they would and would not like something to be *hard as a rock*.
lexical semantics—meanings of words and meanings among words	First-grade students read about two children finding a *chest*. They talk about what this is, then draw and write about a chest they would like to find.
pragmatics—the meanings of words in context	A class reads about *volume* and *pitch* when studying sound. They reflect that *volume* can also mean how much space something takes up, and *pitch* has a different meaning in baseball.
sentential semantics—meanings of phrases and sentences	Students read, "Roger studied the man across from him with scorn." They were unsure whether it was Roger or the man who was scornful.
syntax—how words and phrases are organized	Eighth-grade students read, "The captain heard grumbling among the crew, but he chose to ignore it." They stop to discuss how *grumbling*, a verb, is used as a noun. They add it to their list of gerunds in their learning logs.

Silly Sentences

Grades: K–1

Description

When students create Silly Sentences, they begin with a basic subject-verb pattern, then expand the sentence to include descriptive words and phrases. Students are encouraged to add silly ideas, allowing them freedom to explore language on their terms.

Rationale

During this shared-language activity, the teacher makes suggestions for word or phrase expansions and models how to construct more complex sentences. The teacher scaffolds learning by reading and writing for students, then pointing to the words as students repeat the sentences.

Roles and Responsibilities

Teacher: Writer

- Writes a simple sentence on the board or chart, and reads it aloud.
- Asks questions or makes suggestions for students to expand the sentence.
- Writes and reads students' suggestions.

Student: Sentence Constructor

- Makes suggestions, including silly ones, to construct more complex sentences.

Process

This may be done as a whole class or in small groups. Gather students around the board or chart. Write a simple sentence (such as "Bees buzz."), then point to and read the words you wrote. Be sure to point out the capital letter and end punctuation. Ask students if they can make the sentence more interesting by adding more information. As students make suggestions, rewrite the sentence with their ideas. Point to and read each sentence again, having the student who made the suggestion repeat (read) the sentence after you. Encourage students to add silly ideas that cannot possibly be true.

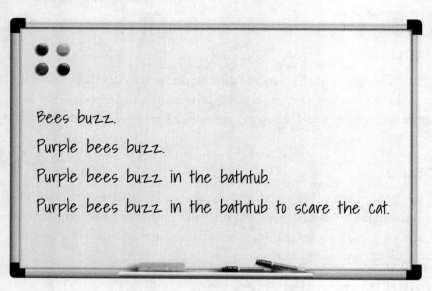

Bees buzz.

Purple bees buzz.

Purple bees buzz in the bathtub.

Purple bees buzz in the bathtub to scare the cat.

Use these shared sentence builder activities to encourage students to expand on their ideas when retelling stories. For example, if a student restates an event, ask them to expand on their idea to explain where or why the event occurred.

Differentiation

If students struggle to come up with ideas, ask guiding questions such as, *Where do bees buzz? What kind of bees are they? What are the bees like?* Add simple pictures to more complex words. In the example, shade the word *purple* with a purple highlighter and draw a picture of a bathtub. Provide copies of the sentences for students to add to their independent reading folders so they can practice reading them on their own.

Same and Different Baskets

Grades: 2–3

Description

Same and Different Baskets is a game-type strategy that has students sort words into two categories: synonyms and antonyms. Students pick a word, then decide if it has a similar or opposite meaning to the word on each of two "baskets," one labeled *synonyms* and the other labeled *antonyms*.

Rationale

Same and Different Baskets helps students build their vocabulary skills. When the baskets are placed where students may easily reference them, students may identify additional words they encounter during reading to add to the baskets. This strategy also provides students with ready lists of valuable words they may use to add clarity to their writing. Same and Different Baskets may be revisited throughout the year for different words. This allows the teacher to strategically target general and academic words students will encounter in text.

Roles and Responsibilities

Teacher: Farmer

- Identifies synonyms and antonyms aligned to words students are encountering in text and writes each one on a fruit-shaped paper cutout.
- Labels each of two "baskets" with a target word and *synonyms* or *antonyms*.

Student: Harvester

- Picks a "fruit," reads and uses the word correctly in a sentence, then identifies the word as a synonym or antonym of the target word.

Process

Identify a target word from a piece of text being used in the classroom. For example, students recently were exposed to the word *elated*. Label each of two baskets as *elated synonyms* and *elated antonyms*. These baskets may be drawn on the board or chart paper or created on a bulletin board, or they may be physical containers. Write six to eight synonyms and six to eight antonyms of *elated*, each on its own fruit-shaped paper cutout. Invite students, one at a time, to pick a fruit, read the word, then use it in a sentence. Then, students place the fruit in the *synonym* or *antonym* basket.

Differentiation

Explicitly teach the terms *synonym* and *antonym*. Encourage students to use these terms when identifying words with similar and opposite meanings. As students read the words, use facial expressions to show what the words mean. After each activity, have students fold a sheet of paper in half, then draw and label a picture with the target word and its synonyms on one side and the antonyms on the other side.

Sentence Scramble

Description

When students participate in a Sentence Scramble, they consider individual words or different parts of a sentence, each written on its own sentence strip or note card, and attempt to place the words or sentence parts in order to make a complete, coherent sentence.

Rationale

Sentence Scrambles give students practice "playing" with syntax and capitalization and punctuation rules. This tactile strategy engages thinking, and it encourages students to rely on their understanding of sentence construction to succeed.

Roles and Responsibilities

Teacher: Sentence Scrambler

- Identifies sentences from text, and writes individual words, phrases, or longer word parts each on its own sentence strip or note card.
- Lays the cards in random order on the table.
- Facilitates discussion.

Student: Sentence Unscrambler

- Reads the words, parts, and phrases.
- Organizes the cards into a complete, coherent sentence.

Process

Locate an expanded sentence from a text the students are currently reading. Use note cards or sentence strips to write individual words, phrases, or clauses, each on its own card. Explain that students should collaborate to organize the cards into a cohesive, complete sentence. Remind students to use capitalization and punctuation rules to help them. Encourage students to reread the words once they order them to be sure the sentence makes sense. Ensure the discussion directly relates to the instruction that supports students' understanding of complex sentences and their parts. **Note:** Use an online tool, such as Scrambled Text Generator or Scrambled Sentence Maker, to aid in scrambling sentences.

Example

The teacher creates word cards using the following sentence from the book *Blackbird Wilderness* by Dani Neiley (2020, 18): "Stella rolled her eyes and pulled out her trusty cell phone to call Mom and Dad, and then it was her turn to look panicked as she remembered there was no service."

to call Mom and Dad	Stella rolled her eyes
and then it was her turn	and pulled out her trusty cell phone
as she remembered	there was no service
to look panicked	

Working as a guided reading group, students manipulate the sentence parts to construct a complete compound-complex sentence from the story. Then students revisit page 18 of the book to determine if the order of the sentence parts is accurate. The group discusses and corrects the sentence as needed.

Differentiation

Begin with just two to four words or phrases, then build to longer, more complex sentences. Write the words, phrases, or parts with puzzle-piece ends that fit together when the sentence is constructed correctly.

Figuratively Speaking

Secondary Grades

Description

Students collaborate to identify and interpret figures of speech as they arise in context, then analyze their roles in the text.

Rationale

Figurative language and figures of speech can be problematic for students when they are reading. By identifying and teaching their meanings in context, teachers can support student comprehension.

Roles and Responsibilities

Teacher: Figures-of-Speech Identifier

- Selects mentor texts with figures of speech, such as euphemisms and oxymorons.
- Plans questions to ask students about the figures of speech in context.

Student: Reader

- Reads texts provided by the teacher.
- Identifies and interprets figures of speech in context.
- Analyzes the role of figures of speech in the text.

Process

Look to your national or state standards to find the types of figures of speech students should know and interpret. When selecting texts, identify examples to discuss. Make notes to yourself about the language you want to discuss, including guiding questions. During reading, stop and discuss the language the author uses. Have students talk with partners or in small groups to first analyze and interpret the language, then share their ideas with the class.

Example

Ninth-grade students read Robert Frost's "Stopping by Woods on a Snowy Evening." Their goal is to determine the theme of the poem and identify lines that support the theme. During the lesson, the teacher says, "*Sleep*, in lines 15 and 16, is a euphemism. This means that the word *sleep* is a kinder word for a harsh idea. What does Frost mean when he writes, 'And miles to go before I sleep'? How does this figure of speech affect the tone of the poem?"

Differentiation

Directly teach domain-specific terms related to figures of speech (and their definitions) to students. Identify figures of speech in context, and give students two options as to their identities. For example, if students read, *moonlight danced on the rippling water*, suggest that this is either personification or a metaphor. Have students explain the meanings of figures of speech they encounter in context in their own words.

Moving Forward: Top Must-Dos

Without an understanding of language structures, students will struggle to comprehend text with increasing complexity. Follow these steps to support student learning of the essential language skills they need to be successful readers and writers.

Provide Supports for Confusing Sentence Structures

Richard Zipoli (2017) discusses four sentence structures that may impede comprehension for both elementary and middle school students. They are sentences with any of the following:

- passive verbs
- adverbial clauses with temporal and causal conjunctions
- center-embedded relative clauses
- three or more clauses

Each of these sentence structures is outlined in figure 4.5. Also listed are suggestions for clarifying understanding.

Figure 4.5—Confusing Sentence Structures and Corrective Strategies

Source of Confusion	Example	Corrective Strategy
passive verb tense	The ball was found by the boy.	Directed questioning: *What was found? Who did the finding?*
adverbial clauses with temporal and causal conjunctions	After dinner, but before they went to bed, the mouse family read a story by the fire.	Sequencing tasks: *What happened first? Next? Last?*
center-embedded relative clauses	Justin, who was always stirring up trouble, blamed his brother for leaving a mess.	Sentence combining activities: *Justin was always stirring up trouble; Justin blamed his brother; Justin left a mess.*

Source of Confusion	Example	Corrective Strategy
three or more clauses	Once the fort was built, the club could begin convening, but only if their leader was present.	Sentence decomposition activities: *Independent clause: The club could begin convening. What had to happen before the club could convene? Under what circumstances could the club convene?*

Teach Syntax and Semantics Using a Logical Scope and Sequence

Language concepts, like math concepts, build on each other. Students cannot learn to comprehend complex sentence structures without first understanding that the essential message is found in the subject and predicate. The addition of phrases, clauses, and figurative language add to the complexity of sentence construction. Each type of phrase and clause serves a purpose, and teachers should provide meaningful instruction to help students understand that. National and state language standards provide specific syntax and semantics skills students should master at each grade level. Some of these skills may flow into reading and writing standards as well.

Teach Syntax and Semantics Explicitly and Systematically

Teachers should not assume that just because students read at a fourth- (or seventh- or ninth-) grade reading level, they can automatically comprehend complex sentence structures. Teachers should provide direct instruction in sentence construction, followed by opportunities for guided and independent practice. Modeling includes using think-alouds to teach specific skills, and underlining or highlighting conjunctions and prepositions that impact meaning. Guided and independent practice may take the form of activity sheets, writing tasks, games, or integrated reading tasks.

Further Considerations

Much of the literature related to language-skill acquisition connects to writing more so than reading. Teachers should consider devoting time to developing and having students practice new language skills as they compose summaries, reports, or reflections, and when they engage in creative writing activities.

Teachers may also use their students' writing as a formative assessment to determine which language skills they lack or for which they may need support. For example, students who regularly use helping verbs incorrectly may benefit from a mini-lesson related to how and when to use these verbs. Then, students may participate in games or other activities to practice identifying and using them. Teachers may continue to support target skills by providing specific, corrective feedback when conferencing with their students about their writing.

My Teaching Checklist

Are you ready to develop students' language skills so they may be successful readers of complex texts? Use this checklist to help you get started!

Developing Language Skills	
Look Fors	**Description**
A variety of complex structures are modeled, and sentence structure is directly taught.	• Begin with simple sentences, then add phrases and clauses. • Be sure students can identify the subject and predicate of complex sentences.
Complex structures in context are taught as the need arises.	• Use mentor texts, novels, content-area texts, or other reading materials. • Ask directed questions to guide student understanding.
Nuances in word meanings are taught.	• Create word maps. • Sort and classify words based on intensity levels.

Chapter Summary

Understanding how *language* works leads to understanding *text*. It begins with how words are constructed to form a sentence, then morphs into the meanings of individual words, phrases, and clauses. Toss in a bit of figurative language, non-literal word choices, and nuanced words, and simple ideas all of a sudden may be expressed in complex sentences that are difficult for students to comprehend. Students must have direct instruction in both syntax and semantics to navigate more complex sentences. This includes teacher modeling and guided and independent practice, both outside of and within context.

Reflection Questions

1. How does the structure of language impact students' comprehension?

2. Explain *syntax* and *semantics* in your own words.

3. What strategies will you use to teach syntax? What strategies will you use to teach semantics?

4. What is a language skill you have helped students develop? How did you do it?

Chapter 5

Text Structures and Verbal Reasoning

From the Classroom

Text structure isn't the easiest to teach nor is it the easiest to learn. As a principal, I regularly visited classrooms to observe learning. One day, I walked into a fifth-grade classroom and something different was happening. The teacher wasn't providing direct instruction on text structure. Instead, students were rifling off different types of questions to engage with the text. Students shouted:

"Does this text structure include a main idea?"

"Is the author trying to prove something?"

"Is there specific evidence that supports the author's purpose?"

"What other ways could this text be interpreted?"

"What is important about this text?"

I looked around the room to see if the students were reading off a list. Then I spotted it: a wall full of question stems from floor to ceiling. These question stems followed Art Costa's Levels of Thinking (2001). It amazed me how these students were engaging in critical thinking by selectively using questions to examine the structure and eventually comprehend the subject matter. I whispered to a student, asking what they were doing. With enthusiasm, the student replied, "We are trying to understand this text. So, we need to figure out what questions can help us understand what we are looking at." I thought to myself, "WOW! Critical questioning to develop an understanding of the way authors organize information in text!"

As the teacher affirmed the type of text structure, the question she posed next was, "What organizer could be associated with this structure?" The kids jumped on it! They turned their heads to the right and looked at the wall of thinking maps and selected their visual. I asked the same student why it was important to have a visual. She said, "So we can organize our ideas. Usually, we will answer questions that we come up with, and sometimes we write about it."

—Kimberly Saguilan
Former Principal
Edward B. Cole Academy
Santa Ana, California

Background Information and Research

Much of the information that students need to comprehend from text isn't in the text at all! Often, students need to draw conclusions, develop inferences, and make logical connections from the information within the text. When understanding is constructed, it can be called *verbal reasoning*. Verbal reasoning refers to the ability to infer, draw conclusions, and understand the text beyond what is explicitly stated. This complex skill requires quite a bit of thinking. Students must first think about the facts or information presented, then think about their own personal experiences and knowledge, and finally combine these two components to construct meaning. This skill set includes classification, determining complex meanings, and reasoning.

> Verbal reasoning refers to the ability to infer, draw conclusions, and understand the text beyond what is explicitly stated. This complex skill requires quite a bit of thinking.

Another complex reading skill that impacts comprehension is identifying and understanding the impact of text structures (Duke and Cartwright 2021). This includes using background knowledge, vocabulary, literacy knowledge, language structures, and verbal reasoning to make sense of a text. When students understand text structures, they are more likely to connect relevant information between sentences, paragraphs, sections, or longer texts. When reading fiction, students must make connections between story elements. For nonfiction, students make connections between pieces of content. In primary grades, this amounts to focusing on text features more so than text structures. Fortunately, **signal words** can clue in the reader to a particular structure. Authors use signal words (also referred to as *transition words*) to provide structure; they guide readers to make connections. In this manner, students use these connections to determine text structure. Once they have identified the structure, students can use it to build meaning from the text.

Verbal reasoning weaves into the Language Comprehension strand of the Reading Rope (Scarborough 2001). As students read text, they encounter words and phrases that allude to other ideas. One integral piece of verbal reasoning is inference. Students must use the words they read and combine them with background knowledge and understanding to **infer**. In addition to making inferences from everyday text, students must learn to do this when they read metaphors, idioms, and other figurative language. (For information about figurative language and its relationship to comprehension, please revisit Chapter 4.)

Verbal Reasoning: Making Inferences

As young readers, students learn to restate what an author says. Teachers guide students to make connections with the text. In this way, students can be more active participants in the reading process by making meaning for themselves. Still, the goal is to have students simply identify key details as the author has written them. They use this *explicit* information to ask and answer questions about the text, to retell stories, or to determine the central message (fiction) or main idea (nonfiction) of the text.

The ability to identify key details based on explicit information is an important stepping-stone to the ability to infer deeper meaning within text. At this point, generally beginning in fourth grade, students learn to add key details to other information to infer meaning. You can see the direct connection between students' own background knowledge and their ability to make inferences.

Amy Elleman and Eric Oslund (2019) recognize inference-making and background knowledge as having a strong effect on comprehension. They cite studies that conclude that inference-making "plays a stronger direct role in comprehension than vocabulary" (4) and that it "is a unique predictor of reading comprehension across developmental stages" (5). Clearly, students need opportunities to think and reflect about what they know and make connections to what they read.

> Many people refer to inference-making as *reading between the lines.*

Making Connections Using Text Features and Structures

One part of constructing meaning is identifying connections between and among the pieces of information within the text, and between and among ideas across texts. Making these connections helps students better understand the content. Transitions help readers make connections among sentences, among paragraphs, and among entire texts. Recognizing these transitions leads students to understand the structure of the text. Additionally, nonfiction texts use **text features** such as headings, captions, and graphics to organize, relay, or reinforce important information. Some text features that students need to understand are listed in figure 5.1.

Figure 5.1—Text Features

Text Feature	Description
table of contents	list of chapters or sections; at the beginning of a book
index	alphabetical list of names and topics, with page numbers showing their location in the text; at the end of a book
glossary	alphabetical list of vocabulary and their definitions; at the end of a book
headings	titles for sections of text within a chapter
bold words	essential terms in bold print within the text
sidebars	short supportive pieces of text, usually boxed, to the side of the main text
captions	titles or brief descriptions of pictures, diagrams, charts, or other visuals
diagrams	drawings showing the appearance or structure of something, or showing how something works
charts and graphs	figures that organize information visually

Text structure is defined as "the ways authors organize information in text" (Seeds of Science/Roots of Reading 2013, para. 1). Instruction in the components of text structure has been shown to improve the comprehension of text. Through exposure and direct instruction using exemplar texts, students can build their knowledge of text structures and practice using them to support their understanding (Hebert et al. 2016; Jones, Clark, and Reutzel 2016). Nell K. Duke, Alessandra Ward, and P. David Pearson (2021) write, "Attention to the structure of the text during reading may provide a helpful scaffold for the syntactic complexity and conceptual density that are characteristic of many written texts" (666). When students understand text features and structures, they have more tools to be able to discover the meaning of text. "Teaching students to recognize the underlying structure of content-area texts can help students focus attention on key concepts and relationships, anticipate what's to come, and monitor their comprehension as they read" (Seeds of Science/Roots of Reading 2013, para. 1).

Determining text structure helps students organize ideas and information, and make connections within and between texts. Doing so leads to better comprehension and more complete text summaries.

Informational texts may be structured in several different ways:

- cause-effect
- comparison
- description
- problem-solution
- sequence of events

Authors use signal words to relate ideas within the text. Common signal words along with graphic organizers that can be used when teaching them are listed in figure 5.2. Students greatly benefit from the use of graphic organizers, which scaffold and support student understanding using visual clues.

Figure 5.2—Common Signal Words to Relate or Connect Ideas

Text Structure	Signal Words	Graphic Organizer
cause-effect	as a result, as a consequence, because, brought about, consequently, due to, for, in order to, led to, since, so, that is why, the effect of, the outcome was, the reason was, therefore	
compare-contrast	also, although, as opposed to, as well as, both, different, however, like, much as, not only…but also, on the contrary, on the other hand, same, similar(ly), too, yet	
description	all, for example, for instance, in addition, in fact, most(ly), some, specifically, such as, to illustrate, too	
problem-solution	answer, challenge, conclusion, dilemma, fortunately, issue, led to, one challenge, problem, question, solved, therefore, trouble, unfortunately	
sequence of events	after, before, during, eventually, finally, first, following, immediately, in the end, last(ly), meanwhile, next, now, then, when, while	

In narrative fiction, students will encounter a range of features that indicate the text type. Most of these texts are identifiable as they have a beginning, middle, and end. Narrative text structure uses the story structure that contains story elements found in figure 5.3. (Graphic organizers may also be helpful in teaching these elements.)

Figure 5.3—Elements of Story Structure

Element	Description/Other Key Terms
character	who is in the story: protagonist, antagonist, static character, dynamic character, and confidante character
setting	time and place where the story happens
conflict	the main challenge to overcome
plot	the narrative structure (basic: beginning–middle–end; complex: exposition–rising action–climax–falling action–resolution)
exposition	background information, including backstories and context
rising action	challenges, conflicts, and complications are introduced
climax	the turning point when tensions in the plot come to a head
falling action	when the tensions begin to dissolve
resolution	sense of closure
parallel plot	includes two or more separate narratives linked by a common character, event, or theme
flashback	scene from past that describes prior events
foreshadowing	a hint of what will come in the story
theme	the "moral of a story" or an analogy (a hidden meaning in the text)

A meta-analysis of the effects of text structure on comprehension clearly shows that proficient readers are able to, among other essential comprehension skills, "make active use of text structure to organize their memory for textual content; they attend to both the external physical organization of the text (e.g., headings, table of contents) and the internal structure of ideas for a better understanding" (Bogaerds-Hazenberg, Evers-Vermeul, and van den Bergh 2020, 436). Conversely, less proficient readers do not rely on text structure to guide their reading.

National and state reading standards offer guidance for instruction. The expectation is that students learn to identify connections between ideas within a single text, then move to making connections between multiple texts.

Making Connections within Texts

Let's dig into using components of text structure by exploring the idea of students making connections within texts. When students are able to identify these connections, they understand that the information in the text is delineated into sentences, paragraphs, and larger portions (such as sections or chapters), and they know how those varying components are related.

One way students do this is by identifying and making connections between individual sentences and paragraphs. Both text features and cue words help students locate information quickly. These are related to the author's purpose and typically provide clues for making meaning. For example, when reading a book about plant growth, students may come across diagrams and illustrations with captions. The visuals support the main text; however, the captions may include additional vital information that is not included in the main text. Each type of feature has its own purpose, helping students identify important information, specific topics, and essential vocabulary words.

As discussed in Chapter 1, texts with high cohesion explicitly provide these connections (Halliday and Hassan, 2014). These texts use words and phrases, often pronouns, that refer to earlier words or phrases, and transition words such as *because*, *therefore*, *finally*, and *in addition*, which effectively "allow information and ideas to be integrated across phrases and sentences" (Castles, Rastle, and Nation 2018, 30).

Making Connections between and among Texts

Students should also develop the skills to make connections between multiple texts, which allow them to comprehend new information by integrating and evaluating it across texts. For example, one text about the Iroquois Confederacy will provide students with facts and information about the purpose of the confederacy, the challenges they faced, and the successes they experienced. Supplementing the text-based information with a detailed map of the region of the Iroquois tribes will help students begin to connect events to specific locations. Analyzing a time line of events will help students organize the information into the meaningful context of time. Reading information and looking at pictures from the time period will support students in better comprehending the nature of this important governing body.

It all begins, well, at the beginning. If students are to make connections between texts, teachers still need to activate and build background knowledge with each text (or type of text). Additionally, they must provide explicit instruction to guide students in determining how the information across texts is connected. Students might identify the structure of each text, discuss how the information compares, record facts from each text, or respond to a thoughtful question about the topic. In the case of the above example, students may write to explain, "How was the Iroquois Confederacy successful?"

Implications for Teaching and Learning

Students may not automatically make inferences when reading. They also may overlook or skip over important text features. Determining text structure helps students organize ideas and information, and make connections within and between texts. Doing so leads to better comprehension and more complete text summaries.

Explicitly Teach Students Strategies to Support Inference-Making

The challenging skill of inference-making requires teachers to extensively model thinking and provide regular opportunities for students to practice making inferences on their own. Teachers can use think-alouds to model pausing when reading to restate what the text says and actively using knowledge and understanding to make inferences. Additionally, teachers can model how to elaborate on ideas presented in texts and examine how text clues lead readers to make reasonable inferences.

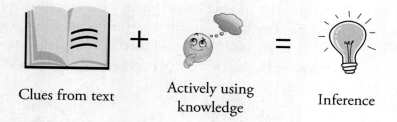

Clues from text + Actively using knowledge = Inference

Making predictions is similar to, but not the same as, making inferences. When students make predictions, they think about what might happen next based on what has already occurred. When students make inferences, they think and consider what the author is trying to tell them based on the information presented.

Inferencing may be done before, during, or after reading. Before reading, students might consider the meaning of the text's title and preview chapter titles to infer how the story might develop. During reading, students can share and discuss their reactions to events or characters' actions. They may jot notes about questions or "a-ha" moments on sticky notes. They might use graphic organizers to analyze characters' actions and story events. After reading, students can revisit questions they have or discuss important events or actions, making inferences based on what happened. They might also revisit their ideas from a pre-reading activity and discuss how their ideas about a particular situation have changed based on events and actions in the story.

Teach Signal Words (Connectors) as Clues to Text Structure

Making connections between content allows students to identify text structure. To connect ideas within text, authors use signal words. (See figure 5.2.) Signal words offer valuable insight into how various concepts and ideas are related within text. When students can identify these signal words, they can relate the information, make the connections, and better comprehend the content. Although students in the primary grades do not necessarily identify text structures per se (they are more focused on identifying and using text features), they are asked to make connections between people, places, events, and ideas within text.

To help students learn signal words, teachers can find texts that include signal words and support content instruction, and use those texts to explicitly teach signal words. Their purpose should be discovered and explored through a range of examples. Teaching students how signal words interact with text will help them when they encounter the words independently.

Students can engage with signal words through sorting, defining their purpose, and creating their own writing that includes signal words. Further, teachers can engage students in authentic opportunities to decipher how signal words are used within text. They can search for them, describe their utility, and share how they informed their understanding. If any texts are missing signal words, teachers will need to provide explicit instruction on how to make in-text connections without them. Additionally, teachers should tell students before they begin reading what type of connection to identify. That sets a clear purpose for reading and focuses attention on relationships between ideas.

Use Graphic Organizers as Tools to Identify Text Structures and Relate Information

Graphic organizers provide students with a structured and explicit manner in which to identify the structure of the text, which then allows them to conceptualize how the information is related (Pyle et al. 2017). Additionally, graphic organizers may be developed quickly for specific reading tasks. For example, teachers can use a Top Hat organizer to have students compare and contrast information as an alternative to the Venn diagram. They may easily pre-label each section, perhaps using headings and subheadings in text, to guide students to connect the correct information. Teachers may also fill in parts of the organizer to support students with learning disabilities. This way, students are directed to specific text, yet they need only find and complete the organizer instead of having to fill in the entire page.

This Top Hat Organizer compares the Middle Ages and the Renaissance Period.

Middle Ages	Renaissance
CE 476 to 14th century	14th to 17th century
Few advances in science and art	Advances in science, philosophy, and art
Also called Dark Ages	Started in Florence, Italy
Bubonic plague	Also called Age of Enlightenment
Crusades	

Both

New inventions

Cathedrals

Expanded trade routes

Key Terms for Teacher Understanding

Term and Definition	Example
inference—conclusion based on both evidence and reasoning	Third-grade students list characters' thoughts, words, and actions in a particular part of a story, then make inferences about the characters' traits based on what they thought, said, and did.
signal words—specific words that transition between (relate) ideas or events	Fifth-grade students read two texts about renewable and nonrenewable resources. They relate ideas between both texts by analyzing how each author compares these two types of resources. They record facts about the resources on a compare-contrast graphic organizer.

Term and Definition	Example
story elements—main components that make up a complete fictional narrative: characters, setting, conflict, plot (includes rising action, climax, falling action), and resolution	A kindergarten teacher reads aloud *The One Day House* by Julia Durango. After reading, the class pages back through the book to identify the main characters, setting, and main events.
text features—all the components of informational or expository text that are not part of the main text: table of contents, index, glossary, headings and subheadings, bold and italicized words, sidebars, pictures and captions, and diagrams and other visual supports	First-grade students read information online about goods and services. They use online menus and icons to identify and restate key facts about them. Then, they draw and label pictures to show examples of each.
text structure—how information in informational or expository text is organized: cause-effect, compare-contrast, description, problem-solution, sequence	Sixth-grade students read about how the tilt of Earth's axis affects weather patterns and seasons. After that, they identify signal words that indicate cause-effect relationships and record these relationships in a cause-effect organizer.

Text Feature Walk

Grades: K–1

Description

A Text Feature Walk is a shared reading strategy similar to a picture or word walk, where students page through an informational book (or scan an informational text) looking for, identifying, and discussing the purpose of various text features. This may be completed as a whole class using an informational Big Book or in small groups using reading texts.

Rationale

A Text Feature Walk allows students to preview the text before reading. This lets students make predictions or connect to prior knowledge. The teacher may draw attention to specific text features and lead a discussion as to their purpose. During reading, the teacher may direct students' attention to specific information in the text feature and help students make connections within the text.

Roles and Responsibilities

Teacher: Facilitator

- Identifies text features to discuss during the Text Feature Walk.
- Plans guiding questions related to text features.

Student: Scanner

- Pages through the text.
- Points to specific text features.
- Answers questions about text features and makes predictions about the content.

Process

Review your national or state standards to determine which text features students are responsible for learning about. Use texts that demonstrate the use of these features. Plan relevant questions to pique interest and activate prior knowledge. For example, "What do you think the arrows on the plant diagram tell us?" or "Which parts of the community in this map are also in our community?" After reading, have students reflect on how conducing a Text Feature Walk before reading helped them make predictions about and better learn the content.

Differentiation

Consider updating a chart that lists specific text features along with examples and their purposes. Refer to the chart as students come across these features in subsequent texts.

Text Feature Scavenger Hunt

Grades: 2–3

Description

Students who participate in a Text Feature Scavenger Hunt page through an informational text independently, with a partner, or as a small group to locate and record various text features. Then, students reflect on how each feature helps them comprehend the text.

Rationale

A Text Feature Scavenger Hunt reinforces the purpose of the features and allows students to reflect on how the features aid comprehension.

Roles and Responsibilities

Teacher: Facilitator

- Provides texts for students to preview.

Student: Hunter

- Examines the text.
- Identifies specific text features.
- Reflects in writing as to the purpose for and usefulness of the features.

Process

Review your national or state standards to determine which text features students are responsible for learning about. Provide students with texts that demonstrate the use of these features. Before reading, have students examine and identify features within the text. Students record the text features they located and describe their purpose in writing. After reading, engage students in a reflective discussion highlighting how the features helped them better understand the content.

Text Feature	Which Page?	Purpose

Differentiation

If you are using an organizer similar to the one shown here, consider listing the text features students should locate or the pages they should review. Provide different options to different students or student pairs, and have students share their findings with the group or class.

Signal Words

Grades: 4–5

Description

Students in the intermediate grades can use Signal Words to help them identify text structures and to make connections within and among texts. Examples of common signal words are included in figure 5.2.

Rationale

When students use Signal Words to determine text structures, they can understand how an author links ideas, shows relationships among ideas, and transitions from one idea to the next.

Roles and Responsibilities

Teacher: Text Presenter

- Chooses a suitable informational text that uses signal words to determine text structure.
- Provides students with an appropriate graphic organizer to record and respond to text.

Student: Signal Word Finder and Text Structure Identifier

- Reads the text and identifies signal words that indicate text structure.
- Records and responds to information on a graphic organizer.

Process

In the example on the next page, fourth-grade students in Florida are learning about the three branches of state and federal government. They read through the text once, then review it again to highlight signal words that show comparisons, drawing from examples on a class anchor chart. The students and teacher work together to list the comparisons in a matrix. Finally, students use the information in the organizer to respond to questions about state government.

	State Government	Federal Government	Both
Executive Branch	governor lieutenant governor state capital	president vice president nation's capital	voters elect representatives carries out laws
Legislative Branch	districts drawn up by population 120 representatives 40 senators state laws	districts drawn up by county lines 435 representatives 100 senators federal laws	makes laws House of Representatives Senate
Judicial Branch	state supreme court is highest court, has 7 judges	U.S. Supreme Court is highest court, has 9 judges	court system

Differentiation

Post and maintain a class anchor chart or bulletin board of signal words for each type of text structure. As students encounter additional words in other texts, add them to the chart. For struggling readers, write statements with related information on note cards for students to organize after reading. This may be done for any text structure students are identifying.

Text Analysis

Secondary Grades

Description

The teacher guides students to analyze how an author develops and refines ideas and claims at the sentence and paragraph levels. With nonfiction, students identify elaboration, examples, details, claims, and evidence to relate content. With fiction, students identify literary techniques such as flashbacks, foreshadowing, or parallel plots to relate events.

Rationale

By identifying a particular literary element (or text structure), students may begin to relate events and determine the correct order of events. This critical-thinking skill (analysis) may be applied across a wide range of other tasks, such as solving problems.

Roles and Responsibilities

Teacher: Facilitator

- Assigns reading material.
- Assigns analysis report.

Student: Analyzer

- Reads assigned material.
- Analyzes text for content or style.
- Writes a text-analysis response.

Process

During literacy class, the teacher assigns students to read one of three short stories. In each story, the author has used a flashback or parallel plot. Students read a story of choice and analyze how the story element affects the sequence of events. Following this, students write a response using specific details to describe how the author uses the literary element for effect.

Differentiation

Provide a paragraph frame to support students as they write their responses. Assign short stories that are written at varying readability levels. Review the definitions of *flashback* and *parallel plot*, and cite examples students have read in class.

Moving Forward: Top Must-Dos

Both making inferences and identifying text structures are complex skills. Students must learn to read critically to analyze information so that they may relate ideas within and among texts. Follow these steps to support student application of the critical reading skills they need to support comprehension.

Model and Teach Strategies to Support Inference-Making

Inferring is not easy. It involves being able to draw connections between what the author states explicitly and the information that is the hidden meaning or understanding. Timothy Shanahan writes, "Written messages—texts—are not so complete or explicit to allow readers to make full sense of them without filling some gaps or making some connections. Authors don't tell everything. They imply an awful lot. Inferences are used to make sense of those implications" (2021a, para. 9). This highlights the need to teach students explicitly how they can identify these spots and make sense of them. Students need to develop the strategy of paying attention to recognize when the text is missing information that they need to fill in. This intentional, active work of reading is highlighted in Nell K. Duke and Kelly B. Cartwright's Active View of Reading Model (2021). What might this instruction look like? Begin by selecting texts that require students to fill in the gaps to completely understand. Read these texts to or with students, and pause when these parts of text come up. Model the process: Stop and think about what the author wants you to know without explicitly stating it. Initially, you will need to plan ahead by marking the text with stopping points. As students begin to recognize the spots themselves, have them restate what the text says explicitly, share the knowledge they bring to the text, and combine this information to make an inference. Post an anchor chart explaining strategies to support inference. Include a simple template students may use to guide their inference-making (see figure 5.4).

> " Written messages—texts—are not so complete or explicit to allow readers to make full sense of them without filling some gaps or making some connections. Authors don't tell everything. They imply an awful lot. Inferences are used to make sense of those implications. "
>
> —Timothy Shanahan (2021a, para. 9)

Figure 5.4—Making Inferences Graphic Organizer

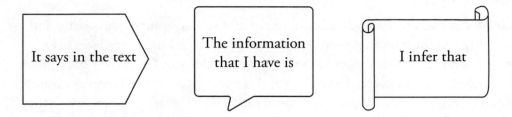

Additionally, use question stems to support students with inferences:

- What information is missing? Where can we get it?
- Why do you think the author told us…?
- What does the author mean when they say…?
- What can you tell about…based on…?
- Why did [this character] [do this]?

Teach Students to Determine the Purpose of Text Features and Text Structures

Directly teach students to identify the purpose and impact of text features and text structures. Before and during reading, be sure students stop and notice the text features. Discuss what information the feature provides and why the author included it there. After reading, have students summarize how the text features support the information and help them better comprehend the content.

Since there are so many different text structures, directly teach each one using a suitable text. Post and refer to an anchor chart listing the text structure and signal words students can use to help them identify it. Before reading unfamiliar text, be sure students preview the text features. These may also provide clues to the text structure. Have students identify signal words during reading that allude to a particular text structure. Provide a suitable graphic organizer for students to complete after reading. This will help them make connections among the content. Finally, follow up with a writing activity where students summarize the text by referencing the relationships among related content.

Use Graphic Organizers to Support Understanding of Text Structures and Parts of Text

Graphic organizers help students make sense of related content and clarify and simplify a lot of information in a concise manner. In doing so, students may better comprehend the information presented in the text, build their background knowledge and vocabulary, and deepen their understanding of complex ideas. Graphic organizers are especially helpful for students in upper grades when they begin to relate information across different texts.

Further Considerations

There is exceptional power in supporting all students in engaging actively with text and the nuances found within it. Students need to be able to identify different text structures. However, the ultimate goal is for students to comprehend the information. Identifying text structures is a means to an end, not an end in itself. Plan for instruction that extends students' knowledge and understanding of text structures to ensure they are connecting that knowledge in a way that increases their comprehension. Provide follow-up lessons on identifying signal words and text structures by having students use completed graphic organizers to answer relevant comprehension questions. This way, students are using the graphic organizers to relate information and ultimately comprehend the text, which in turn adds to their content knowledge.

> There is exceptional power in supporting all students in engaging actively with text and the nuances found within it. Students need to be able to identify different text structures.

My Teaching Checklist

Are you ready to develop students' inferencing skills and teach them to identify text structures so they may be successful, critical readers of complex texts? Use this checklist to help you get started!

Verbal Reasoning and Text Structures	
Look Fors	**Description**
Strategies to support making inferences are modeled and taught.	• Use mentor texts and think-alouds. • Have students identify the gap the author left within the text. • Allow students to identify the explicit information, the knowledge and understanding that supports it, and the inferences that can be made.
Text features and text structures are taught.	• Identify text features in text, and discuss how they improve comprehension. • Teach and use signal words that relate information within texts.
Graphic organizers are used to support instruction.	• Use organizers that match the structure of the text. • Have students use the organizer they completed to summarize content.

Chapter Summary

Students must be able to make inferences when they read because the messages authors leave are not always explicitly stated. Students learn and use ideas embedded "between the lines" when they read critically. Teaching this complex skill requires effective and regular modeling and practice.

Knowing how to use text features supports student understanding of the text. When students use text features, they may make predictions, anticipate what they will read about, and identify important topics. Recognizing text structures helps students identify relationships among information. They may make connections between ideas and build their understanding of facts, vocabulary, and important concepts.

Reflection Questions

1. How is making inferences an essential skill for comprehension?

2. Why is teaching students to identify and use text features equally as important as teaching them to comprehend text?

3. How does the use of graphic organizers help students determine text structure?

4. How will you use ideas presented in this chapter to support student comprehension?

Chapter 6

Reading Comprehension Strategies

From the Classroom

Having been a struggling reader myself, I'm keenly aware of how multifaceted the process of reading truly is. Long after we master the ability to decode letter-sound relationships, we continue to face many challenges that call on our higher-order thinking skills. It is with this complexity in mind that I jump at any opportunity to teach an overarching, active literacy strategy involving "tracking one's thinking" when reading.

In fact, when I was serving as a director of literacy, I was supporting a driver's education teacher at one of our local high schools. The teacher was frustrated with finding time to teach much of the content from the textbook because of the many class hours dedicated to mandatory hours of driving practice. However, some essential knowledge is needed for students to become successful drivers and, of course, pass a written exam. So how could this teacher, with little instructional time, increase students' focus on the most important aspects of the text and best utilize every minute of classroom time? While many approaches may come to mind, one that was successful in this drivers' ed classroom was a simple Code the Text routine.

First, we set a purpose for reading the text. Since the topic was "managing intersections," finding relevancy was fairly easy to achieve with the question, "*Why* do we need to read this passage?" Students quickly made comments like, "So we don't crash" and "No one wants to pay for a ticket." Next, we modeled how to "code the text" by pausing during reading the first paragraph aloud to demonstrate our own thinking about key ideas or questions we might have. For example, after the first section on right-hand turns, we commented, "At first, it feels funny to turn on a red light, but there are times it is allowed, so we begin to get used to it." To display our thinking further, we drew a star on a sticky note and placed it next to key ideas and did the same with a question mark for any ideas we did not understand.

Finally, the students practiced this process with partners for about 10 minutes. We answered any questions and guided the partners, if necessary. The students were then directed to complete the Code the Text activity independently at home that evening.

And guess what? The next day, the teacher was surprised at how much conversation came about as students shared their questions and key ideas! Misunderstandings were easily pinpointed and addressed much more efficiently because of the tangible way in which students' thoughts were labeled and posted right on pages of the text. The teacher later reflected that the days of simply assigning a reading were long gone and how exciting it was to know exactly which ideas the students were struggling with and which were understood more completely!

—Lisa Callahan
Former Director of Literacy
Community Unit School District 200
Wheaton, Illinois

Background Information and Research

What is comprehension? This book is focused on what the science says about how students can develop the skills and strategies to successfully understand what they read. Each chapter in this book breaks down parts of how text works so that instruction can support comprehension and bring meaning to what students read. This chapter both synthesizes the information presented in previous chapters and offers a fresh look at teaching specific strategies to help students monitor their own comprehension and be active and engaged readers of both fiction and nonfiction texts.

Comprehension *is* the ultimate purpose of reading text. Whatever the reading model examined and followed, teachers have long understood that ultimately, reading instruction boils down to supporting students in understanding what they read so they are able to use the information to learn, grow, and develop greater understanding. Throughout this book, we have examined each of the five key strands that Hollis Scarborough (2001) identified as *Language Comprehension*: background and content knowledge, vocabulary, language structures, verbal reasoning, and literacy knowledge. We have been considering how to support all students navigating text. As students become increasingly strategic about collectively using and applying their knowledge related to these strands, they become skilled readers capable of reading and comprehending complex texts independently.

"Teaching" Comprehension

In this chapter, we will carefully dive into explicit instruction with comprehension strategies. Duke and Cartwright (2021) state that "comprehension strategy use has been shown to predict reading ability even beyond word recognition and language comprehension" (S32). Reading Rockets (n.d.) defines comprehension simply as "the understanding and interpretation of what is read" (para. 1). However, teachers know the process of comprehension is quite complex and varies greatly among readers.

The Simple View of Reading (Gough and Tunmer 1986) identifies the skill of reading as the product of word recognition and language comprehension. The first of these, decoding (word recognition), is explored in depth in *What the Science of Reading Says about Word Recognition* by Jennifer Jump and Robin Johnson (2023). However, simply being able to decode words (or read fluently) does not necessarily mean students will comprehend text. As Duke, Ward, and Pearson (2021) remind us, "As important as foundational word-reading and bridging skills are to reading comprehension, research has shown that they are not sufficient for strong comprehension" (665). Word recognition and reading fluency are only part of the reading comprehension puzzle.

> Deep thinking is where real comprehension occurs. In order for students to think deeply about what they are reading, they must learn to think critically about the words they read.

The second part, language comprehension, has been widely explored throughout this book. Knowledge and vocabulary, along with strong command of syntax and semantics, support students as they work through text. Print concepts and genre understanding paired with verbal reasoning skills and a comprehensive grasp of text structure provide students with strong avenues to understanding text. They bridge what they know with information presented in texts, making connections within texts and between and among texts. This, however, only really happens when students are able to engage *with* the text. Deep thinking is where real comprehension occurs. In order for students to think deeply about what they are reading, they must learn to think critically about the words they read. This requires analysis based on the content of the text. In order to read critically, students must be active readers, mindful of their personal engagement with the content.

Daniel T. Willingham (2007) recognizes the challenges that teachers face when teaching students to think critically. He indicates that metacognitive strategies "make critical thinking more likely" (17). He also notes that using metacognitive strategies "requires domain knowledge and practice" (13).

> "Strategies like monitoring, self-questioning, visualizing, comparing the text with prior knowledge, identifying text organization, and so on are all intentional, purposeful actions that are effective in improving comprehension or recall.
>
> —Timothy Shanahan
> (2018, para. 7)

With that acknowledged, let's explore several avenues for teaching students to think about (comprehend) text. First, we will consider instructional strategies teachers may use during reading or content-area instruction. Secondly, we will consider ways to support students with strategies to rely on their own thinking (**metacognition**) when reading independently.

Instructional Strategies Before, During, and After Reading

Teachers can support students throughout the reading process to ensure they develop the knowledge and strategies that lead to the skills to understand text. To ensure that each lesson that involves text includes instruction that supports comprehension, plan for instructional components before, during, and after reading. Many of these ideas are a coordination of the strategies and skills that have been shown to support students throughout this book. Consider the supports in figure 6.1. Remember to use the gradual release of responsibility model to support students as they move to conducting the work of comprehending on their own.

Figure 6.1—Strategies that Support Comprehension Before, During, and After Reading

Time Period	Strategies
Before Reading	• Complete an anticipation guide. • Preview the text (features, key words, etc.). • Make predictions. • Read the first line of each section. • Discuss/list what you already know.
During Reading	• Identify connectors and text structures. • Build a concept map or other graphic organizer. • Reflect on predictions. • Visualize events and concepts. • Identify gaps and infer.
After Reading	• Summarize or retell. • Use headings to ask and answer questions. • Respond in writing to reading.

Questioning Strategies

Teachers ask questions during and after reading texts to gauge how well students understand the content. An examination of what kinds of questions are asked and the purpose of the questions is an important consideration. Shanahan cautions that comprehension questions should not focus on specific standards and skills, but instead should be "on the basis of the texts themselves" and "should lead kids to think deeply about a text and to come away with a coherent and lasting memory of its content and aesthetic qualities" (2018, para. 25). Planning a sequence of questions that allows students to

> **Stop and Think!** Where have you previously read about before-, during-, and after-reading strategies in this book?

develop a breadth of understanding improves overall comprehension and supports students as they work to understand text on their own.

Brandon Cline (n.d.) regards asking questions as "the most powerful tool we possess as teachers" (para. 1). He acknowledges that "mastering the art of asking good questions is a lifelong pursuit" (para. 2) and proposes a four-step process for learning to ask better comprehension questions. These steps are outlined in figure 6.2.

Figure 6.2—Steps to Developing Better Comprehension Questions

Step	Explanation
Perform a Question-Asking Audit	Ask a colleague to observe a lesson and tally the questions you ask into two categories: low level and high level (see figure 6.3).
Build a Question-Asking Toolkit	Make a list of the kinds of questions you might ask students.
Cultivate Your Question-Asking Style	Reflect on how you ask questions (tone, word choice, phrasing, nonverbal cues, wait time).
Further Refine Your Technique	Plan questions before each lesson and organize them in a sequence that makes sense.

Sometimes teachers ask questions "on the fly" or rely on teacher's guides to pose questions about texts. However, in doing so, teachers may find that "such questions have phrasing problems, are not organized in a logical sequence, or do not require students to use the desired thinking skills," according to the Center for Innovation in Teaching and Learning (n.d., para. 1). Therefore, planning questions to ask during reading is an essential part of preparing a more complete lesson.

Questions can be divided into two categories: *low level* and *high level*. Low-level questions are often referred to as "right there" questions. Students can find the answers directly in the text. The questions can often be answered with one word or phrase. Students generally need to recall information to answer them. High-level questions require a bit more thought. Students must look beyond the obvious, through interpretation and inference of events or story elements to answer them. These responses require a deeper explanation. Douglas Fisher and Nancy Frey (2013b) indicate that close, analytical reading of text should allow for questions that keep students closely tied to the text, rather than being "encouraged to answer questions that too soon take them away from the reading to their own experiences" (57). Questions should be planned to allow students to engage richly with the text.

Additionally, questions can also be categorized as *closed* or *open*. Closed questions have an expected and typically short response. Open questions have more than one acceptable answer. Figure 6.3 displays how questions can overlap both categories, using the topic of a bicameral government system.

Figure 6.3—Question Matrix

Question Type	Low Level	High Level
Closed	What is a bicameral government system?	How does the government system of Canada compare to that of the United Kingdom?
Open	Which countries have a bicameral government system?	What are some advantages and disadvantages of a bicameral government system?

Another important part of asking questions is responding to student answers. Teachers have several ways to respond to the answers students provide. Whether students are offered positive reinforcement or are probed to offer more details or clarify their answers, they should be given ample opportunities to dig back into the text for additional reasoning, for evidence, or to clarify misunderstanding.

Questioning has long been an effective means of checking for student understanding of reading selections. With careful planning and attention to content, teachers can use questions to guide students to better comprehend what they read.

Comprehension Self-Monitoring Strategies

Since the goal of reading is to comprehend, and we want students to learn to comprehend texts independently, they need to learn how to self-monitor their reading. Self-monitoring is a process of metacognition. Merriam-Webster (n.d.-b.) defines *metacognition* as "awareness or analysis of one's own learning or thinking processes." When students self-monitor, they recognize when something does not make sense. They monitor their own internal exchange of ideas between what they know and what the text says. They think to themselves, "I don't understand this," and figure out how to resolve the disconnect.

Castles, Rastle, and Nation (2018) refer to comprehension monitoring strategies, which are "typically defined as the collection of strategies or skills used to evaluate one's own comprehension, to identify when comprehension has gone astray, and, where appropriate, to repair any misunderstanding" (32).

Following are methods students may utilize to monitor their own comprehension of text.

Annotations

As an adult reader, Jen often finds herself jotting notes in the margins of books and articles that she reads. One would know how deeply she reads a text by the number of sticky notes hanging off the side. Students too can benefit from annotating text—taking notes right on the text. When students engage with annotations, they can begin by learning basic markings that allow them to mark up their text with a pencil. These markings provide students with adequate space to recall information that they have read, use the annotations to respond to questions, discover areas of confusion, and identify evidence that supports their responses to questions (Fisher and Frey 2013a).

Annotations are useful tools that provide a way for students to interact with text. Students need extensive support through modeling and practice opportunities to learn and develop the skill of annotating text. Modeling provides students with a clear pathway to using annotations to support the comprehension of text. How students annotate should match their changing developmental needs. Annotations can become more complex as students develop their understanding and familiarity with using them and navigating complex text. Nancy Frey and Douglas Fisher (2013) note, "In primary grades annotations are confined to underlining key points and circling unfamiliar words. As students progress into the intermediate grades, teachers begin to add other marks" (32).

Students can use annotations throughout the reading process, during multiple reads, highlighting various discoveries. Annotations can also be tailored to meet the specific needs of students. With the ultimate purpose of annotations supporting comprehension of text, clear purpose combined with flexibility allow for the highest utility of annotations. Doug Lemov, Colleen Driggs, and Erica Woolway (2016) articulate a range of purposes for marking text. These include identifying evidence, summarizing, paraphrasing, rereading, noting key ideas or themes, key vocabulary, objective, and final writing connection. Students can use annotations in various ways to meet specific needs. Different texts will invite students to examine them in nuanced ways, changing how annotations support their understanding. Providing students with a versatile annotation toolbox will give them a foundation that supports their reading journey.

Figure 6.4—Common Text Codes

Symbol	When to Use It
underline	when you discover an important point or main idea
circle	when you encounter key words or phrases
*	when you reach an important statement or discovery
?	when you are confused or wondering something
margin notes	when something you are reading can be rewritten or paraphrased to help you understand

Fix-Up Strategies

Students can self-monitor their comprehension using **fix-up strategies**. These have utility when students realize something in the text isn't making sense to them. Like other comprehension strategies explored in this chapter, teachers begin by modeling. As they read with small groups or the whole class, teachers may begin to call on students to choose a fix-up strategy when comprehension breaks down.

Teachers can guide students to discover when comprehension begins to break down using effective questioning strategies.

Students may use fix-up strategies as they occur in context. Students can practice using annotations or sticky notes near the text where they do not understand something so as to not interrupt the flow of reading. Then, they may return to the question(s) they have at the end of a reading selection. By reading on, students may discover the answer to their initial questions.

Common fix-up strategies are listed in figure 6.5 along with self-talk questions and remarks that students may be thinking when they read.

Figure 6.5—Fix-up Strategies for Students

Problem	Self-Talk	Possible Fix-up Strategies
A word does not make sense.	• I don't know what this word means. • Is this word important for understanding the information/story?	• Use diagrams or other visuals to figure out the word's meaning. • Reread to see if the author defined the word or offered a synonym in context. • Look up the word in a glossary or dictionary.
A sentence does not make sense.	• This sentence does not make sense. • How does this sentence "fit in" with the rest of the text?	• Reread it slowly. • Reread it aloud. • Reread the sentences before and after it. • Relate this sentence to another sentence in the text.

Problem	Self-Talk	Possible Fix-up Strategies
A paragraph does not make sense.	• This paragraph is confusing. • What information is important to know in this paragraph?	• Reread it slowly. • Reread it aloud. • Use visuals to support the information. • Revisit the purpose for reading. • Reread the heading for the paragraph's section. • Relate this paragraph to other information in the text. • Think about how the information relates to what I already know.

Feed Up, Feed Back, Feed Forward

Another strategy that supports students' active reading is the Feed Up, Feed Back, Feed Forward model proposed by Douglas Fisher and Nancy Frey (2016, 88–89). The main components of this model are explained in figure 6.6. Essentially, this formative assessment strategy uses teacher observation of student learning to make adjustments to future instruction.

Figure 6.6—Feed Up, Feed Back, Feed Forward Instructional Strategy

Step	Purpose
Feed Up	• Set and clarify the purpose (goal) for learning. • Plan readings, projects, investigations, and assessments to help students meet the goal.
Feed Back	• Inform students of their progress toward meeting the goal. • Constructively respond to student work.
Feed Forward	• Modify instruction based on student work. • Provide additional meaningful tasks for students who need them.

Science Example: Third-grade students are learning about the relationships among the sun, the moon, and Earth. Goal: understand that the sun is a star, Earth is a planet that orbits the sun, and the moon orbits Earth. Students read various texts and articles about Earth that describe these relationships. During a sorting activity, the teacher observes five students who incorrectly label each object. He meets with these students and provides language frames for students to complete: _____ *is a* _____. _____ *orbits* _____. The group works to correctly complete each sentence using the words *sun, Earth, moon, planet,* and *star*.

Social Studies Example: Sixth-grade students are learning about the production and distribution of goods in ancient civilizations. Goal: understand how the production and distribution of agricultural goods compare between Egypt and Mesopotamia. Students read informational texts and analyze maps and diagrams related to this topic. When completing a comparison graphic organizer, the teacher observes about half the students struggling to formulate ideas. She begins asking questions to support student learning: "Which river flooded each year in Egypt? Which rivers flooded each year in Mesopotamia? How did the civilizations benefit from the floods?"

Implications for Teaching and Learning

Teachers should not assume students, even fluent readers, will automatically comprehend the texts they read. Shanahan et al. (2010) recommend teachers follow these steps to improve students' reading comprehension.

Teach Reading Comprehension Strategies

Explicit instruction of reading comprehension strategies (such as the following) has a positive effect on comprehension:

- activating background knowledge or predicting
- questioning
- visualizing
- monitoring, clarifying, or fixing up
- making inferences
- summarizing or retelling

According to Shanahan et al. (2010), "different strategies cultivate different kinds of thinking" (12). They suggest teachers model how to use the strategies, and gradually release responsibility for using the strategies to students.

Teach Students to Use Text Structure as a Tool

Showing students how to identify text structures aids overall comprehension. This idea was discussed in detail in Chapter 5. Recommendations include the following:

- show students how to identify and connect parts of narrative texts
- provide instruction in common structures of informational texts

Shanahan et al. (2010) suggest using a variety of literature to demonstrate how texts within a single genre can have different structures. They also recommend providing students with increasingly more complex texts to apply their understanding of text structure knowledge.

Plan for Focused Discussions on a Text's Meaning

Discussing what has been read during and after reading allows students to reflect on the information in the text, clarify confusing information, and build knowledge in a collaborative setting. Discussions may be led by the teacher or by students. The teacher may have a series of questions for the class or group to consider, or students may devise their own questions to discuss. When working in groups, students should rotate group roles (see figure 6.7) so all students have a chance to participate in a different manner. Questions should focus on what students should know and remember about the story or informational text.

Figure 6.7—Discussion Group Roles

| Discussion Leader | Timekeeper | Note Taker |
| Wordsmith | Presenter | Clarifier |

Intentionally Select Texts that Support Comprehension Development

We want students to become skillful, independent readers. To get there, we need to provide texts in class that offer adequate opportunities to build knowledge and vocabulary as well as ensure students have access to rich, complex text. Students may face text that is challenging for them to comprehend; thus, we need to provide support to guide their comprehension. This may be accomplished by setting a clear purpose, using strategies shared earlier in this book, and providing some sort of outline or organizer for students to complete to help manage the information.

Establish an Engaging and Motivating Context for Instruction

It stands to reason that if students (or anyone for that matter) are interested in something, they will be more likely to participate or get involved. This is true for reading, too! Duke, Ward, and Pearson (2021) elaborate on the research-based notion that motivation improves comprehension. They cite research that identifies three main strategies that act to motivate student interest in a topic and the text or texts about it:

- conducting hands-on activities
- offering choices
- providing process-oriented feedback

At times teachers are anxious to jump right to the reading selection. It's worth the time to motivate readers before they begin reading.

Key Terms for Teacher Understanding

Term and Definition	Example
annotations—symbols and notes about a text selection, written in margins or on sticky notes	A sixth grader is reading about the Tarahumara people from Chihuahua. While reading, the student underlines an important detail about different kinds of footraces.
fix-up strategies—actions readers may take to monitor their own reading comprehension	While Emma is reading about the Revolutionary War, she can't make sense of one part of the text. She rereads the paragraphs in this section and realizes she was unclear about the sequence of events.
metacognition—the act of thinking about one's own thinking	While reading an article about Rosie the Riveter, an eighth-grade student thinks about the reasons why women went into the workforce during the WWII era. She asks herself, "Were women entirely motivated by patriotism, or was it something else?"

Self-Monitoring

Grades: K–1

Description

When students self-monitor, they listen to themselves read and stop to think about what they have read. When teachers teach students in the early grades to monitor their reading, they will likely do so during read-aloud or shared reading mini-lessons. Additionally, teachers will model their own self-monitoring for students to then mimic when they are asked to explain how they monitor their own reading.

Rationale

Self-monitoring requires students to develop self-talk about the text. In this manner, they may become active readers, identifying when words don't make sense and when meaning breaks down. They may rely on their own thinking to understand the author's message, along with main ideas and details about a topic.

Roles and Responsibilities

Teacher: Reader and Thinker

- Reads text aloud.

- Stops to think about their own reading.

- Models how to reread or read more slowly to understand the text.

Student: Reader and Thinker

- Reads or rereads text.

- Mimics teacher's examples for self-monitoring for meaning.

Process

Select a text to read aloud to students. Plan stopping points to think aloud, asking questions such as, "What picture do I have in my mind about [this event]? Can I retell the story so far? Does this word make sense?" Reread the text, perhaps more slowly, then clarify your understanding by saying something like, "Oh, now I know how [this event] fits into the story. I see why [this character] [did this]. I was not sure what an *aquarium* was, but I can tell from the pictures that it is a place with lots of fish."

Differentiation

Post pictures or illustrations in a reading nook that remind students to think about their reading. Have students share their thinking with one another. Provide drawing materials for students to explain what they read by illustrating the main message or main ideas.

Shown here is an anchor chart the teacher may post to reference when modeling self-monitoring strategies and for students to reference during independent reading. Note: This strategy does not encourage students to guess words or meaning, rather, it allows the practice of self-monitoring while engaging with text.

Somebody Wanted But So Then

Grades: 2–3

Description

This strategy is used during or after reading. It provides a framework for students to summarize a story. Although it is more often used with fiction, it can also be used to summarize the goal, motivation, or conflict of historical people and events.

Rationale

Somebody Wanted But So Then helps students identify main ideas and cause-effect relationships, generalize, compare characters, and consider different points of view. The language frame guides students to analyze who did what, and why.

Roles and Responsibilities

Teacher: Modeler

- Identifies a suitable text to summarize.
- Reads the text, then uses the language frame to summarize the text.

Student: Summarizer

- Reads the text, then uses the language frame to summarize the text.

Process

Teachers should model this strategy for students several times, allowing for gradual release of responsibility to students. Post the language frame. Read a story or text, then use the frame to summarize events.

Somebody... Who was the main character?	
Wanted... What did the main character want?	
But... What was the problem?	
So... How did the characters try to solve the problem?	
Then... How was the problem solved?	

This example summarizes *Julius, the Baby of the World* by Kevin Henkes (1990).

> Lily wanted Julius to disappear, but his parents thought he was "the baby of the world," so Lily did mean things to him. Then her cousin insulted him, and Lily realized she loved Julius.

Differentiation

Allow students to annotate the text with the keywords: Somebody, Wanted, But, So, Then. Call on different students to offer responses to each part of the frame. Have students work with partners to summarize the text using the frame. Provide answers for students to place in the appropriate location in the frame.

SQ3R

Grades: 4–5

Description

SQ3R is a comprehension strategy usually used with nonfiction text. It is an acronym for *survey, question, read, recite, review*. Students first preview text features (survey), then turn the headings into questions (question). After they read each section, students stop and try to answer their questions from memory (recite). After finishing the reading selection, they review every question to be sure they can answer it.

Rationale

The SQ3R strategy requires students to fully engage with the text, think about what they are reading, and be personally responsible for comprehending the content.

Roles and Responsibilities

Teacher: Text Selector

- Identifies texts with appropriate text features.
- Models the strategy before having students try it on their own.

Student: Surveyor, Questioner, Reader, Reciter, Reviewer

- Surveys text features and uses headings to write questions about the content.
- Reads and answers their own questions.
- Reviews the entire text selection and reflects on their own understanding of the content.

Process

Choose a chapter from a content-area textbook or other text (article or reading text) with an adequate number of headings. Model how to survey the text, considering bold words, captions, diagrams, and other visuals. Read each heading, and turn it into a question. Read one section of text at a time, then pause and use the information to answer the question you asked before reading that section. Continue reading and answering questions one section at a time. At the end of the text selection, review all the questions again.

Differentiation

Have students use the question words (*who*, *what*, *where*, *when*, *why*, and *how*) to form their questions. Allow student pairs to survey, question, read, and recite together. Assign texts to pairs or small groups of students that are a better match to their instructional reading levels.

Seminar

Secondary Grades

Description

In a Seminar discussion, students actively participate to understand ideas, issues, and values presented in a text. The Seminar allows time for each student to prepare information garnered from learning and share it through a structured discussion. According to Mary Davenport (2016), direct instruction about what makes a good seminar is the first step in the process.

Rationale

By exploring thoughts about text through discussion, students may more deeply understand the ideas and values presented by the author. Students consider their own points of view and reflect on others' points of view about issues and principles as they support their interpretations of a text.

Roles and Responsibilities

Teacher: Initial Leader

- Identifies rich texts that lend themselves to deep discussions.
- Plans and models how to lead a discussion about the content and themes.

Student: Discussion Leader

- Poses questions for group discussion.
- Supports other students to contribute constructively to the discussion.

Process

Establish and practice expectations regularly. Model and teach students to be discussion leaders, and gradually release this responsibility to them. Choose a text that crosses content areas and offers real-world connections. Plan text-based, open-ended questions related to the content and themes. Also plan follow-up questions that require students to quote text, expand on others' ideas, and keep the conversation going. Seat students in a circle, and pose an initial question for students to discuss. Try not to insert your own ideas, and instead encourage students to share and explore their own and each other's ideas based on the reading material.

Differentiation

Set up an inner and outer circle (also referred to as a *fishbowl*), where students in the center contribute to the discussion, and students along the perimeter listen and restate the students' ideas once the discussion has ended. After each session, have students reflect on what worked well and what they need to change next time to improve the discussion. Record students' ideas on a chart to review before the next seminar.

Moving Forward: Top Must-Dos

The point of reading is to make meaning from text—to comprehend. The suggestions in this chapter offer various ways to use direct instruction to show students how to comprehend texts. In addition, we looked at self-monitoring strategies students can use when reading independently. Moving forward, consider the following key ideas.

Provide Explicit Instruction in Comprehension Strategies

Begin by selecting high-quality texts that lend themselves to modeling and teaching specific comprehension strategies. The texts should also intentionally be chosen to build knowledge and vocabulary. Remember to broaden students' exposure to multiple genres. Decide on a strategy for the focus of each lesson. Model how to read the text and use the strategy. Gradually release responsibility for using the strategy and comprehending the text to students.

Teach Students to Think about What They Read While They Read

Thinking about one's thinking while reading is an essential process in engaging with and comprehending text. By using metacognitive strategies, students can recognize what does and does not make sense. Metacognition begins before reading when students consider their personal background knowledge and make predictions about the text. During reading, students can engage in self-talk, reflecting on the information and using comprehension strategies to "fix up" what does not make sense. After reading, students may reflect on the text as a whole and revisit and reread sections that may have been confusing or incomprehensible. Teachers can remind students that when they read, they need to think about the words, the message, and the organization of the information in order to make sense of the text.

Use Graphic Organizers to Support Comprehension

To help students make sense of information, they may record facts, information, and ideas in useful graphic organizers. These help students organize related information in a visual manner and manage a lot of information, which helps them construct meaning and build knowledge.

Further Considerations

There are many instructional moves that will support students' comprehension as they work through all types of text. Students need explicit and modeled instruction to support their development of comprehension strategies. They need numerous opportunities to engage with the actions that help them determine the meaning of text. However, this important work should not overshadow the science-backed understanding that knowledge and vocabulary are also key aspects in developing student comprehension. Rather, the two should complement one another through thoughtful instructional planning that provides collections of worthy texts that build knowledge and vocabulary, paired with intentional instruction in strategies that support comprehension. Marissa Filderman et al. (2022) articulate the findings from a meta-analysis examining the effects of various interventions on third to twelfth graders' comprehension. The findings clearly demonstrate the continued thread from the science of reading. Students need explicit strategies and extensive opportunities to engage with information, building knowledge to find the most success in comprehending text.

My Teaching Checklist

Are you ready to develop students' comprehension skills so they may be successful readers of complex texts? Use this checklist to help you get started!

Comprehending Text	
Look Fors	**Description**
Comprehension strategies are directly taught.	• Use appropriately complex texts, and model and teach students how to use comprehension strategies. • Gradually release responsibility for comprehension to students.
Students are reminded to think about their thinking when reading.	• Model how you use your own thinking when reading. • Record metacognitive strategies on an anchor chart to refer to when students read.
Graphic organizers are used to support comprehension.	• Match the style of the organizer to what students are to comprehend. • Show students how to use organizers to organize information and show relationships among concepts and ideas.

Chapter Summary

Comprehension is a multifaceted process. This book has been written strategically to support each component while simultaneously keeping the end in mind. Vocabulary and background knowledge are critical pieces as students begin to comprehend new texts. Students must also reason and make connections within and across texts. And they must be active readers, thinking about what they are reading when they are reading it. To help students put it all together, teachers must directly teach students how to comprehend what they are reading. This includes the use of comprehension strategies that may be used before, during, and after reading.

Reflection Questions

1. Which comprehension strategies will you teach to students in the future? How will you know if students can use the strategy when they read independently?

2. Why is metacognition an important part of reading?

3. How does self-monitoring of reading relate to developing critical thinking skills?

Chapter 7

Selecting Relevant Texts: Find the Mirrors and Windows

by Carrie Eicher
Port Charlotte, Florida

> Students must see themselves in the texts, including their cultures,
> identities, interests, experiences, desires and future selves.
>
> —Gholdy Muhammad (2020, 146)

If I asked you to recall a text you encountered recently (or historically) that, for one reason or another, lit you up and made you feel as if it had been written for or about you, could you do it? If so, or if not, why? Consider what it was about that text that reflected who you knew yourself to be or who you wanted to be in the future. Reading affords us the opportunity to recognize ourselves and our experiences, and to feel connected to and understand perspectives and experiences different from our own. This connection is vital to reading comprehension yet can be incredibly difficult, especially when students' lives, cultures, and languages differ from those they encounter in texts on a regular basis. By using culturally responsive texts that accurately reflect students' cultural and linguistic selves, teachers provide the critical link between prior knowledge and texts, connecting texts directly to students' own lives and the lives of their peers. Culturally responsive texts are an essential component of any literacy program if students are to make connections between what they read and what they already know and think deeply about what they have read.

According to Tanya Christ, a professor at Oakland University, it is critical for students to have the opportunity to read culturally relevant books because they provide an advantage in terms of performance outcomes. "When students read books with more culturally relevant experiences, they were 16 percent more likely to make personal connections between the book and their own lives" (Cho, Christ, and Liu 2022, para. 8). Equally important, using texts that allow students to put themselves in someone else's shoes is a powerful tool for developing empathy, providing a window into cultures, languages, and experiences different from their own.

Considerations for Choosing Relevant Texts

Stories that resonate, validate, and affirm the identities and experiences of readers are what Sharroky Hollie, founder of the Center for Culturally Responsive Teaching and Learning, calls "culturally and linguistically responsive texts" (2018). Culturally responsive texts are those in which students can find themselves, their families, and their communities reflected and valued.

When identifying and using texts that are culturally responsive, teachers must be selective, because not all texts that appear diverse are culturally responsive. It is important to be aware of different types of culturally responsive texts and know what to look for when selecting books that are culturally responsive. When learners do not see themselves in the texts they encounter (read, watch, or listen to), or when they encounter negative stereotypes or inaccuracies about their cultures, languages, or communities, they may feel that their stories or experiences don't matter. Texts that feel as if they are always about someone else, or tell our story in inaccurate ways, turn us off and tune us out. Examining texts for accuracy, realistic images and illustrations, believable characters, and authentic language is a great place to start. Below, you will find additional information on three types of text (Hollie 2018).

- A **culturally authentic** text illuminates the authentic cultural experiences of a particular group—whether it addresses religion, socioeconomic status, gender, ethnicity, nationality, sexual orientation, or geographic location. The language, situations, and illustrations must depict culture in an authentic manner.

- **Culturally generic** texts feature characters of various racial identities but contain few and/or superficial details to define the characters or storylines. Culturally generic texts tend to focus on mainstream cultural values but with the use of nonmainstream characters. Many culturally generic texts qualify as "multicultural."

- **Culturally neutral** texts feature characters of "color," but the stories are drenched with a traditional or mainstream theme, plot, and/or characterization. These types of texts should be avoided. There are exceptions, of course, however it is important to avoid using texts that appear to be culturally authentic but are not.

Culturally Authentic (CA) Texts

Culturally authentic texts illuminate the authentic, nuanced (deep), and accurate cultural and linguistic experiences of particular cultural groups or Rings of Culture (religion, socioeconomic status, gender, ethnicity, nationality, orientation, or age), using language, situations, and images that depict culture and language in a genuine, native manner.

Culturally Generic (CG) Texts

Culturally generic texts feature characters of various racial identities, but unlike culturally authentic texts, contain only superficial cultural details to define the characters or story lines in a responsive manner.

Culturally Neutral (CN) Texts

Culturally neutral literature features characters and topics of "diversity" but includes content that is drenched with traditional or mainstream themes, plots, characterizations, and/or generalizations.

Culturally neutral informational texts are devoid of culture or may include tokenistic portrayals of race or culture and avoid addressing authentic issues.

Source: Management Guide, *Culturally Authentic and Responsive Texts: A Collection Curated by Dr. Sharroky Hollie, Kit Levels K–6*, published by Teacher Created Materials.

Developing Literacy with Relevant Texts

Being intentional about text selection is key to honoring the identities and experiences of students. When teachers use culturally responsive texts, students have a better understanding of the books, and, as a result, they become more engaged in their reading, their enjoyment and interest increase, and they become motivated to read more. Comprehension and interpretation can prove challenging for students who have not been exposed to the same cultural experiences as their peers and for those students who have a limited linguistic background or exposure to the language of the text.

As Sharroky Hollie (2018) notes in *Culturally Responsive Teaching and Learning, Second Edition*, culturally responsive texts vary in their level of responsiveness, and knowing the differences among several types is crucial. Many quality texts that build literacy are culturally responsive to a degree, yet texts that are culturally authentic are the preferred type because they illuminate the authentic, accurate, and nuanced cultural experiences of a particular cultural group.

Cultural background can influence comprehension depending on how students interpret meaning. Students who read a text that is more culturally familiar to them will recall between 20 and 30 percent more than students who are unfamiliar with the cultural references in the text (Ricker 2016).

Culturally responsive texts help students understand who they are and where they come from by illuminating their nuanced experiences, providing validation and affirmation, telling students that their stories matter, and showing them possibilities of who and what they can be. Using culturally responsive texts draws on the cultural knowledge, prior experiences, and identities of the reader to make learning more appropriate and effective for them. Additionally, when students are given the opportunity to engage authentically with key concepts and ideas within culturally responsive texts, they will experience a deeper connection to and comprehension of the text.

Engaging Authentically

How students engage with the text is as important as the text you choose. **BeYou** (**Be Engaged Your Own** Unique Way) is an acronym I developed in partnership with Dr. Hollie when I was coaching teachers across the country in the implementation of culturally and linguistically responsive teaching and learning. I frequently encountered teachers using culturally responsive texts, but the instructional methodology, specifically classroom management strategies, tended to be traditional. Traditional methodology on what behavior is or is not acceptable in the classroom often does not consider students' cultural behaviors and resulting learning needs. This can create disengagement and misunderstanding, specifically for underserved learners, and result in decreased connection to the content and learning experience. *BeYou* is a call to action for adjusting instruction, ensuring students can be who they are at school culturally and linguistically. When students are given the opportunity to be collaborative, sociocentric, dynamic in their attention span, and engaged in kinesthetic learning (for example), they are more likely to engage authentically and therefore deepen their learning.

Student engagement is also an important consideration when assessing student comprehension of a text. What opportunities have students been given to discuss key concepts and communicate relevance, make inferences, or ask questions when constructing meaning? Does the text mirror the students' lived experiences, cultures, or languages? Are students able to draw on their funds of knowledge, tapping into their cultural interactional styles and ways of sharing information? When students are given the opportunity to engage authentically with key concepts and ideas within the text, they will experience a deeper connection to and comprehension of the text. Reading activities, like read-alouds and discussion protocols, can promote interpretation of the text through the interaction between the reader and the text (Wallace 1992) and thus play a vital role in schema activation in order to comprehend and interpret the text better (Chen and Graves 1995; Grabe and Stoller 2002).

Consider the following questions as you reflect on the ways you ask students to engage with culturally responsive texts:

- Are students asked to discuss the key concepts within the text? How?
- What structures do you currently use to facilitate student discussion?
- What literacy activities do you use to promote interpretation of the text?

Next Steps

Involve Students in Evaluating Texts

One way to determine whether books are culturally responsive (ideally culturally authentic) is to involve students in evaluating them. Using a rubric, students can rate each text on several criteria including the setting, socio-cultural factors, and the language characters use. By discussing students' responses, teachers can evaluate whether a book is culturally responsive for a particular group of students. As students grow in their familiarity of accurate, nuanced portrayals, they can become advocates for culturally authentic text and identify when a text is, in fact, perpetuating stereotypes, generalizing, or devoid of culture entirely.

Incorporate Multilingual Activities

Multilingual activities, such as those with a visual or realia component, can give students additional ways to connect with and demonstrate comprehension of a text and benefit from their lived experiences. Encouraging multilingual learners to use their home languages in conversations around a text can build comprehension and engagement with the text.

Watch for Texts that Require Significant Background Knowledge or New Vocabulary

Offering students a choice of several reading options around a central theme or content objective can help them find a text that aligns to their reading identity while also increasing student agency. Additionally, utilizing vocabulary tools such as a personal dictionary or thesaurus can create routines for developing understanding and comprehension of unfamiliar academic vocabulary.

Choose Joy

When selecting culturally responsive books, choose books that reflect a variety of experiences and ensure that readers see themselves portrayed positively in situations that reflect everyday humanity. Joyful books remind children of all identities that their happiness and well-being matter.

Reading and examining texts that illuminate the experiences, contributions, and perspectives of various cultural groups can help young children develop a sense of belonging and identity. Rudine Sims Bishop (1990) states that books should be windows into the realities of others, not just imaginary worlds, and books can be mirrors that reflect the lives of readers. I would bet that the story you recalled earlier resonated with you because either the story or characters mirrored an aspect of your life, identity, or experiences or it created a window into a world different from your own. You felt seen, understood, or compelled, and it moved you! We often seek mirrors in texts, and our students are craving texts that speak to them, open up new understandings and possibilities, and create that moment of recognition and affirmation for them.

Carrie Eicher provides professional development training for school districts, teachers, and educational trainers. Previously, Carrie worked with Dr. Sharroky Hollie as a consultant and coach at the Center for Culturally and Linguistically Responsive Teaching. Carrie started her career in education as a lower elementary teacher, then became an instructional coach, dean of academics and instruction, and finally, an assistant principal.

References

AdLit: All About Adolescent Literacy. n.d. "Classroom Strategies: Frayer Model." Accessed March 14, 2022. adlit.org/in-the-classroom/strategies/frayer-model.

Archer, Anita L. 2011. *Explicit Instruction: Effective and Efficient Teaching*. New York: Guilford Press.

Ardoin, Scott P., Katherine S. Binder, Tori E. Foster, and Andrea M. Zawoyski. 2016. "Repeated versus Wide Reading: A Randomized Control Design Study Examining the Impact of Fluency Interventions on Underlying Reading Behavior." *Journal of School Psychology* 59: 13–38. doi.org/ 10.1016/j.jsp.2016.09.002.

Aronow, Robin, and K. Bannar. n.d. "Semantics: Thematic Roles." LinguisticsNetwork. Accessed March 14, 2022. linguisticsnetwork.com /semantics-thematic-roles.

Beck, Isabel L., Margaret G. McKeown, and Linda Kucan. 2013. *Bringing Words to Life*. New York: Guilford Press.

Bellisario, Gina. 2014. *Choose Good Food! My Eating Tips*. Minneapolis: Millbrook Press.

Binder, Katherine S., Nicole Gilbert, Cheryl Lee Cote, Emily Bessette, and Huong Vu. 2016 "Beyond Breadth: The Contributions of Vocabulary Depth to Reading Comprehension Among Skilled Readers." *Journal of Research in Reading* 40 (3): 333–343. doi.org/10.1111/1467-9817.12069.

Bishop, Rudine Sims. 1990. "Mirrors, Windows, and Sliding Glass Doors." *Perspectives: Choosing and Using Books for the Classroom* 6 (3): ix–xi. The Ohio State University.

Bogaerds-Hazenberg, Suzanne T. M., Jacqueline Evers-Vermeul, and Huub van den Bergh. 2020. "A Meta-Analysis on the Effects of Text Structure Instruction on Reading Comprehension in the Upper Elementary Grades." *Reading Research Quarterly* 56 (3): 435–462. doi.org/10.1002/rrq.311.

Bradley, Timothy J. 2013. *Danger in the Desert*. Huntington Beach, CA: Teacher Created Materials.

Castles, Anne, Kathleen Rastle, and Kate Nation. 2018. "Ending the Reading Wars: Reading Acquisition from Novice to Expert." *Psychological Science in the Public Interest* 19 (1): 5–51. doi.org/10.1177/1529100618772271.

Center for Innovation in Teaching and Learning, University of Illinois. n.d. "Questioning Strategies." Accessed March 14, 2022. citl.illinois.edu/citl-101 /teaching-learning/resources/teaching-strategies/questioning-strategies.

Cervetti, Gina N. and Elfrieda H. Hiebert. 2018. "Knowledge at the Center of English/Language Arts Instruction." *The Reading Teacher* 27 (4): 499–507. doi.org/10.1002/trtr.1758.

Chen, Hsiu-Chieh, and Michael F. Graves. 1995. "Effects of Previewing and Providing Background Knowledge on Taiwanese College Students' Comprehension of American Short Stories." *TESOL Quarterly* 29 (4): 663–686. doi.org/10.2307/3588168.

Cho, Hyonsuk, Tanya Christ, and Yu Liu. 2022. "Recognizing Emergent Bilingual Parent-Child Dyads' Funds of Identity through Their Discussions about Culturally Relevant Text." *Journal of Language, Identity & Education* (1–16). doi.org/10.1080/15348458.2021.2004893.

Clay, Marie M. 1989. "Concepts about Print in English and Other Languages." *The Reading Teacher* 42 (4): 268–276. jstor.org/stable/20200110.

Clay, Marie M. 1993. *An Observation Survey of Early Literacy Achievement.* Portsmouth, NH: Heinemann.

Cline, Brandon. n.d. "The Power of Questions." Chicago Center for Teaching and Learning. Accessed March 14, 2022. teaching.uchicago.edu/resources/teaching -strategies/asking-effective-questions.

Costa, Arthur L. 2001. *Developing Minds: A Resource Book for Teaching Thinking*, 3rd Edition. Alexandria: ASCD.

Davenport, Mary. 2016. "Socratic Seminars: Building a Culture of Student-led Discussion." *Edutopia*. September 22, 2016. www.edutopia.org/blog/socratic -seminars-culture-student-led-discussion-mary-davenport.

Duke, Nell K., and Kelly B. Cartwright. 2021. "The Science of Reading Progresses: Communicating Advances Beyond the Simple View of Reading." *Reading Research Quarterly* 56 (S1): S25– S44. doi.org/10.1002/rrq.411.

Duke, Nell, Alessandra Ward, and P. David Pearson. 2021. "The Science of Reading Comprehension Instruction." *The Reading Teacher* 74 (6): 663–672. doi. org/10.1002/trtr.1993.

Durango, Julia. 2017. *The One Day House.* Watertown, MA: Charlesbridge.

Ehri, Linnea C. 1995. "Phases of Development in Learning to Read Words by Sight." *Journal of Research in Reading* 18 (2): 116–125. doi. org/10.1111/j.1467-9817.1995.tb00077.x.

Ehri, Linnea C., and Sandra McCormick. 1998. "Phases of Word Learning: Implications for Instruction with Delayed and Disabled Readers." *Reading and Writing Quarterly* 14 (2): 135–163. doi.org/10.1080/1057356980140202.

Ehri, Linnea C., and Margaret J. Snowling. 2004. "Developmental Variation in Word Recognition." In *Handbook of Language and Literacy: Development and Disorders*, edited by C. Addison Stone, Elaine R. Silliman, Barbara J. Ehren, and Kenn Apel, 433–460. New York: Guilford Press.

Elleman, Amy M., and Eric L. Oslund. 2019. "Reading Comprehension Research: Implications for Practice and Policy." *Policy Insights from the Behavioral and Brain Sciences* 6 (1): 3–11. doi.org/10.1177/2372732218816339.

Fabbri, Michela. 2020. *I Am a Capybara*. Hudson, NY: Princeton Architectural Press.

Ferlazzo, Larry. 2020. "The Whys and Hows of Activating Students' Background Knowledge." *Education Week*, June 15, 2020. edweek.org/teaching-learning /opinion-the-whys-hows-of-activating-students-background-knowledge/2020/06.

Filderman, Marissa J., Christy R. Austin, Alexis N. Boucher, Katherine O'Donnell, and Elizabeth A. Swanson. "A Meta-Analysis of the Effects of Reading Comprehension Interventions on the Reading Comprehension Outcomes of Struggling Readers in Third Through 12th Grades." *Exceptional Children* 88 (2): 163–84. doi.org/10.1177/00144029211050860.

Fisher, Douglas, and Nancy Frey. 2013a. "Annotation: Noting Evidence for Later Use." *Principal Leadership* 13 (6): 49–52.

Fisher, Douglas, and Nancy Frey. 2013b. "Close Reading." *Principal Leadership* 13 (7): 57–59.

Fisher, Douglas, and Nancy Frey. 2016. "Feed Up, Back, Forward." In *On Formative Assessment: Readings from Educational Leadership*, edited by Marge Sherer. ascd.org/publications/books/116065/chapters/Feed-Up,-Back,-Forward.aspx.

Fisher, Douglas, Nancy Frey, and John Hattie. 2016. *Visible Learning for Literacy*. Thousand Oaks, CA: Corwin.

Frey, Nancy, and Douglas Fisher. 2013. *Rigorous Reading: 5 Access Points for Comprehending Complex Texts*. Thousand Oaks, CA: Corwin.

Gough, Philip B., and William E. Tunmer. 1986. "Decoding, Reading, and Reading Disability." *Remedial and Special Education* 7 (1): 6–10.

Grabe, W., and L. F. Stoller. 2002. *Teaching and Researching Reading*. Harlow, England: Pearson Education.

Gustafson, Jon. 2019. "Robust Vocabulary Instruction." *Peers and Pedagogy* (blog), September 30, 2019. achievethecore.org/peersandpedagogy/robust-vocabulary-instruction.

Halliday, M. A. K., and Ruqaiya Hasan. 2014. *Cohesion in English*. London: Routledge.

Hanson, Susan, and Jennifer F. M. Padua. n.d. *Teaching Vocabulary Explicitly*. Effective Instructional Strategies Series. Pacific Resources for Education and Learning. Accessed March 14, 2022. files.eric.ed.gov/fulltext/ED585172.pdf.

Harmon, Janis, and Karen Wood. 2018. "The Vocabulary-Comprehension Relationship Across the Disciplines: Implications for Instruction." *Education Sciences* 8 (3): 101. doi.org/10.3390/educsci8030101.

Hattan, Courtney. 2019. "Prompting Rural Students' Use of Background Knowledge and Experience to Support Comprehension of Unfamiliar Content." *Reading Research Quarterly* 54 (4): 451–455. doi.org/10.1002/rrq.270.

Hebert, Michael, Janet J. Bohaty, J. Ron Nelson, and Jessica Brown. 2016. "The Effects of Text Structure Instruction on Expository Reading Comprehension: A Meta-Analysis." *Journal of Educational Psychology* 108 (5): 609–629. doi.org/10.1037/edu0000082.

Henkes, Kevin. 1990. *Julius, the Baby of the World*. New York: Greenwillow Books.

Hervey, Sheena. 2013. *A Beginner's Guide to Text Complexity*. Generation Ready. generationready.com/wp-content/uploads/2021/04/Beginners-Guide-to -Text-Complexity.pdf.

Hiebert, Elfrieda. 2013. "Core Vocabulary and the Challenge of Complex Text." In *Quality Reading Instruction in the Age of Common Core Standards*, edited by Susan B. Neuman and Linda B. Gambrell, 149–161. Newark, DE: International Reading Association.

Hoban, Russell. 1964. *Bread and Jam for Frances*. New York: Harper Collins.

Hollie, Sharroky. 2018. *Culturally and Linguistically Responsive Teaching and Learning, Second Edition*. Huntington Beach, CA: Shell Education

International Literacy Association. 2018. "The Power and Promise of Read-Alouds and Independent Reading." Literacy Leadership Brief. Newark, DE: Author.

Jackson, Robin R., and Allison Zmuda. 2014. "Four (Secret) Keys to Student Engagement." *Educational Leadership* 72 (1): 18–24.

Jiban, Cindy. 2020. "Let's Talk Equity: Reading Levels, Scaffolds, and Grade-Level Text." *Teach. Learn. Grow* (blog), June 25, 2020. nwea.org/blog/2020/equity -in-reading-levels-scaffolds-and-grade-level-text.

Jones, Cindy D., Sarah K. Clark, and D. Ray Reutzel. 2016. "Teaching Text Structure: Examining the Affordances of Children's Informational Texts." *The Elementary School Journal* 117 (1): 143–169. doi.org/10.1086/687812.

Jump, Jennifer, and Robin Johnson. 2023. *What the Science of Reading Says about Word Recognition*. Huntington Beach, CA: Shell Education.

Jump, Jennifer, and Hillary Wolfe. 2023. *What the Science of Reading Says about Writing*. Huntington Beach, CA: Shell Education.

Kelley, Michelle J., and Nicki Clausen-Grace. 2010. "Guiding Students Through Expository Text with Text Feature Walks." *The Reading Teacher* 64 (3): 191–195. doi.org/10.2307/40961980.

Kilpatrick, David A. 2015. *Essentials of Assessing, Preventing, and Overcoming Reading Difficulties*. Hoboken, NJ: John Wiley & Sons.

Lemov, Doug, Colleen Driggs, and Erica Woolway. 2016. *Reading Reconsidered: A Practical Guide to Rigorous Literacy Instruction*. San Francisco: Jossey -Bass.

López-Escribano, Carmen, Susana Valverde-Montesino, and Verónica García-Ortega. 2021. "The Impact of E-Book Reading on Young Children's Emergent Literacy Skills: An Analytical Review." *International Journal of Environmental Research and Public Health* 18 (12): 6510. doi.org/10.3390/ijerph18126510.

Loveless, Becton. n.d. "Learning to Read to Read to Learn. Myth or Reality?" *Education Corner* (blog). Accessed March 14, 2022. www.educationcorner.com/learning-to-read-to-read-to-learn.html/.

Merriam-Webster. n.d.-a "Language." *Merriam-Webster.com Dictionary*. Accessed May 21, 2022. www.merriam-webster.com/dictionary/language.

———. n.d.-b "Metacognition." *Merriam-Webster.com Dictionary*. Accessed May 21, 2022. www.merriam-webster.com/dictionary/metacognition.

———. n.d.-c "Tradition." *Merriam-Webster.com Dictionary*. Accessed May 21, 2022. www.merriam-webster.com/dictionary/tradition.

Moats, Louisa Cook. 2020a. *Speech to Print: Language Essentials for Teachers*. Baltimore: Paul H. Brookes.

Moats, Louisa Cook. 2020b. "Teaching Reading Is Rocket Science." *American Educator*. Summer, 2020.

Muhammad, Gholdy, and Bettina L. Love. 2020. *Cultivating Genius: An Equity Framework for Culturally and Historically Responsive Literacy*. New York: Scholastic.

National Center on Early Childhood Development, Teaching and Learning. n.d. "Book Knowledge and Print Concepts." Accessed March 14, 2022. eclkc.ohs.acf.hhs.gov/sites/default/files/pdf/no-search/dtl-pla-book-knowledge-print-concepts.pdf.

National Reading Panel (U.S.) and National Institute of Child Health and Human Development (U.S.). 2000a. *Report of the National Reading Panel: Teaching Children to Read: An Evidence-based Assessment of the Scientific Research Literature on Reading and Its Implications for Reading Instruction*. Bethesda, MD: U.S. Dept. of Health and Human Services, Public Health Service, National Institutes of Health, National Institute of Child Health and Human Development.

Neiley, Dani. 2020. *Blackbird Wilderness*. Huntington Beach, CA: Teacher Created Materials.

NGSS Lead States. 2013. *Next Generation Science Standards: For States, By States*. Washington, DC: The National Academies Press.

Ogle, Donna M. 1986. "K-W-L: A Teaching Model That Develops Active Reading of expository Text." *The Reading Teacher* 39 (6): 564–570. jstor.org /stable/20199156.

Parlett, Rachael. n.d. "An Easy Strategy to Encourage Your Students to Read a Variety of Genres." *The Classroom Nook* (blog). Accessed March 14, 2022. classroomnook.com/blog/reading-genres.

Pimentel, Sue. 2018. "Why Doesn't Every Teacher Know the Research on Reading Instruction?" *Education Week*, October 26, 2018. edweek.org/teaching -learning/opinion-why-doesn't-every-teacher-know-the-research-on-reading -instruction/2018/10.

Pyle, Nicole, Ariana C. Vasquez, Benjamin Lignugaris/Kraft, Sandra L. Gillam, D. Ray Reutzel, Abbie Olszewski, Hugo Segura, Daphne Hartzheim, Woodrow Laing, and Daniel Pyle. 2017. "Effects of Expository Text Structure Interventions on Comprehension: A Meta-Analysis." *Reading Research Quarterly* 52 (4): 469–501. doi.org/10.1002/rrq.179.

Rasinski, Timothy, Nancy Padak, Rick Newton, and Evangeline Newton. 2020. *Building Vocabulary with Greek and Latin Roots*, 2nd ed. Huntington Beach, CA: Shell Education.

Reading Rockets. n.d. "Comprehension." Accessed March 14, 2022. readingrockets .org/helping/target/comprehension.

Ricker, Joe. 2016. "How a Student's Background Affects Reading Comprehension." Study.com. study.com/academy/lesson/how-a-students-background-affects- reading-comprehension.html.

Ricketts, Jessie, Robert Davies, Jackie Materson, Morag Stuart, and Fiona J. Duff. 2016. "Evidence for Semantic Involvement in Regular and Exception Word Reading in Emergent Readers of English." *Journal of Experimental Child Psychology* 150: 330–345.

Robb, Laura. 2002. "The Myth of Learn to Read/Read to Learn." *Instructor* 111 (8): 23–25. Accessed February 25, 2022. scholastic.com/teachers/articles /teaching-content/myth-learn-readread-learn.

Scarborough, Hollis S. 2001. "Connecting Early Language and Literacy to Later Reading (Dis)abilities: Evidence, Theory, and Practice." In *Handbook for*

Research in Early Literacy, edited by S. Neuman and D. Dickinson, 97–110. New York: Guilford Press.

Sedita, Joan. 2016. "Academic Vocabulary." *The Keys to Literacy* (blog), March 8, 2016. keystoliteracy.com/blog/academic-vocabulary.

Seeds of Science/Roots of Reading. 2013. "Teaching Text Structure: Help Students Identify Signal Words." September 27, 2013. seedsofsciencerootsofreading .wordpress.com/2013/09/27/teaching-text-structure-help-students-identify-signal -words.

Seidenberg, Mark S. 2017. *Language at the Speed of Sight.* New York: Basic Books.

Seifert, Deena. 2015. "Breadth and Depth of Vocabulary Knowledge." *InferCabulary* (blog), May 11, 2015. infercabulary.com/breadth-and-depth-of -vocabulary.

Shanahan, Timothy. 2018. "Where Questioning Fits Comprehension: Skills and Strategies." Reading Rockets: Shanahan on Literacy (blog), June 1, 2018. readingrockets.org/blogs/shanahan-literacy/where-questioning-fits -comprehension-instruction-skills-and-strategies.

Shanahan, Timothy. 2021a. "What Does It Take to Teach Inferencing?" Reading Rockets: Shanahan on Literacy (blog), August 7, 2021. readingrockets.org /blogs/shanahan-literacy/what-does-it-take-teach-inferencing.

Shanahan, Timothy. 2021b. "Why Your Students May Not Be Learning to Comprehend." Reading Rockets: Shanahan on Literacy (blog), March 7, 2021. readingrockets.org/blogs/shanahan-literacy/why-your-students-may-not-be -learning-comprehend.

Shanahan, Timothy, Kim Callison, Christine Carriere, Nell K. Duke, P. David Pearson, Christopher Schatschneider, and Joseph Torgesen. 2010. "IES Practice Guide: Improving Reading Comprehension in Kindergarten Through 3rd grade." (NCEE 2010-4038). Washington, DC: National Center for Education Evaluation and Regional Assistance, Institute of Education Sciences, U.S. Department of Education. ies.ed.gov/ncee/wwc/Docs/PracticeGuide /readingcomp_pg_092810.pdf.

Smith, Reid, Pamela Snow, Tanya Serry, and Lorraine Hammond. 2021. "The Role of Background Knowledge in Reading Comprehension: A Critical Review." *Reading Psychology* 42 (3): 214–240. doi.org/10.1080/02702711.2021.1888348.

Smithsonian Institution. n.d. "OurStory: Winning the Vote for Women: Who Represents You?" Accessed March 14, 2021. amhistory.si.edu/ourstory/pdf /suffrage/suffrage_represents.pdf.

Snow, Pamela C. 2021. "SOLAR: The Science of Language and Reading." *Child Language Teaching and Therapy* 37 (3): 222–233. doi. org/10.1177/0265659020947817.

Stahl, Steven A., Victoria Chou Hare, Richard Sinatra, and James F. Gregory. 1991. "Defining the Role of Prior Knowledge and Vocabulary in Reading Comprehension: The Retiring of Number 41." *Journal of Reading Behavior* 23 (4): 487–508. doi.org/10.1080/10862969109547755.

Tyson, Kimberly. 2013. "No Tears for Tiers: Common Core Tiered Vocabulary Made Simple." dokumen.tips/documents/no-tears-for-tiers-common-core-tiered -vocabulary-made-simple-notearsfor.html/.

University of Queensland. 2017. *Deep Learning through Transformative Pedagogy: Expert Perspectives*. www.youtube.com /watch?v=vLUFCxl5Zb4&t=251s/.

Victoria State Government Education and Training. 2020. "Literacy Teaching Toolkit: Concepts of Print." education.vic.gov.au/school/teachers /teachingresources/discipline/English/literacy/readingviewing/Pages /litfocusconceptsprint.aspx.

Vulchanova, Mila, Evelyn Milburn, Valentin Vulchanov, and Giosuè Baggio. 2019. "Boon or Burden? The Role of Compositional Meaning in Figurative Language Processing and Acquisition." *Journal of Logic, Language, and Information* 28: 359–387.

Wagner, Jennifer. n.d. "What Is Semantics?" ielanguages.com. Accessed March 14, 2022. ielanguages.com/semantics.html.

Wallace, Catherine. 1992. *Reading*. Oxford: Oxford University Press.

Wexler, Natalie. 2019. *The Knowledge Gap: The Hidden Cause of America's Broken Education System—and How to Fix It*. New York: Penguin/ Random House.

Willingham, Daniel T. 2007. "Critical Thinking: Why Is It So Hard to Teach?" *American Educator* Summer 2007: 8–19. aft.org/sites/default/files/periodicals/ Crit_Thinking.pdf.

Willingham, Daniel. 2016. "Knowledge and Practice: The Real Keys to Critical Thinking." Knowledge Matters Issue Brief #1, March 2016. knowledgematterscampaign.org/wp-content/uploads/2016/05/Willingham-brief.pdf.

Zapata, Angie, Monica Kleekamp, and Christina King. 2018. "Expanding the Canon: How Diverse Literature Can Transform Literacy Learning." *Literacy Leadership Brief.* Newark, DE: International Literacy Association.

Zipoli, Richard P. Jr., 2017. "Unraveling Difficult Sentences: Strategies to Support Reading Comprehension." *Intervention in School and Clinic* 52 (4): 218–227.

Glossary

academic vocabulary—words generally used in academic dialogue and text; Tier 2 words

activate background knowledge—trigger students' knowledge about a topic using a stimulus

annotations—symbols and notes about a text selection, written in margins or on sticky notes

background knowledge—collective and combined knowledge gained through study, experiences, interactions, and instruction

breadth of vocabulary knowledge—how many words a person has in their vocabulary; a general understanding of terms

build background knowledge—provide essential prerequisite knowledge to expand on the topic

deep knowledge—integration of previous knowledge with new knowledge to understand underlying principles

depth of vocabulary knowledge—the level of understanding of terms; being able to explain and relate a term to a specific and unique context

domain-specific vocabulary—words specific to a particular topic, subject, or concept; Tier 3 words

figurative language—words and phrases used non-literally for effect

fix-up strategies—actions readers may take to monitor their own reading comprehension

genre—category or type of text differentiated by format, style, and topic

inference—conclusion reached based on both evidence and reasoning

informational text—one category of nonfiction that informs readers about a particular topic

lexical semantics—meanings of words and meanings among words

literature—text in the form of fictional prose, drama, or poetry

metacognition—the act of thinking about one's own thinking

pragmatics—the meanings of words in context

print awareness—also referred to as concepts of print; beginning reading skills related to how books are organized and how text within books shares a message

read-along—instructional strategy where the teacher guides students to read aloud with them (choral read)

read-aloud (noun)—a text the teacher reads to students, modeling aloud how to read with purpose and meaning

read-aloud (verb)—instructional strategy where the teacher reads text aloud to students to model appropriate reading skills

relational reasoning—an executive function that supports ability to see meaningful patterns in information

robust vocabulary instruction—activities that engage students with words regularly and in varying contexts

sentential semantics—meanings of phrases and sentences

shared reading—an interactive reading experience shared between the teacher and students

signal words—specific words that transition between (relate) ideas or events

story elements—main components that make up a complete fictional narrative: characters, setting, conflict, plot (includes rising action, climax, falling action), and resolution

superficial knowledge—information that is obvious

syntax—how words and phrases are organized

text coherence—the unity of ideas within text

text cohesion—how elements in the text are structurally tied together

text features—all the components of informational or expository text that are not part of the main text: table of contents, index, glossary, headings and sub-headings, bold and italicized words, sidebars, pictures and captions, and diagrams and other visual supports

text structure—how information in informational or expository text is organized: cause-effect, compare-contrast, description, problem-solution, sequence

wide reading—reading several texts (perhaps different genres or with different text structures) about a topic

word collocations—vocabulary that uses two or more words to communicate an idea

Index